GUILTY WHEN BLACK

ISBN 978-1-952320-58-3 (Paperback)
Guilty When Black

The pages that follow synthesize what I learned over the course of five years from hundreds of sources. In most cases, descriptions and dialogue that appear in the book are taken directly from the recollections of the family and witnesses, from newspaper accounts, court documents, fire reports, autopsies, law enforcement records, and personal first-hand accounts. In some cases, I have taken the license of approximating dialogue for the purpose of maintaining the narrative. These instances are totally consistent with the character of the people involved as my interviews and research revealed them to be, and wholly true to the events as they unfolded. Events and opinions provided in this book represent those of the people involved and do not reflect those of the author or editors. In select cases, the names of individuals have been changed at their request.

It is up to the reader to research these topics further and determine if what is written is factual. The author disclaims any liability to any party for any loss, damage, or disruption caused by errors or omissions, whether such errors or omissions result from negligence, accident, or any other cause.

Yorkshire Publishing
4613 E. 91st St,
Tulsa, OK 74137
www.YorkshirePublishing.com
918.394.2665

Printed in the USA

GUILTY WHEN BLACK

One girl's journey down the twisted road of injustice and the atrocities of female incarceration

Carol Mersch

TULSA

Contents

"Denial is the heartbeat of racism."

Ibram X. Kendi

"How to Be an Antiracist"

Preface

Room 413, Tulsa County Courthouse

SOMETHING about the case drew me in.

On June 23, 2014, I made my way to the fourth floor of the Tulsa County Courthouse to attend a District Court arraignment in a criminal case against a young black woman—the State of Oklahoma vs. Miashah Moses—a troubling case with racial undertones.

Seven months earlier, Miashah, 23, was charged by Tulsa District Attorney Tim Harris on two counts of second-degree murder in the fiery deaths of her two young nieces, Noni, 4 years old, and Nylah, 18 months old. Harris alleged that Moses's actions were "imminently dangerous" and showed a "depraved mind" when she fixed the children dinner and left them unattended for eight minutes to take out the trash.[1]

I ventured into Judge James Caputo's courtroom that Monday at 9:00 and took a seat in the gallery. The Moses case was delayed, and Caputo called a recess, which put me on a bench outside his courtroom to wait. A large group of black people were gathered there, among them a tall striking woman seated next to me with tight braids laced close to her head.

I had no idea who this woman was but learned in the short time sitting next to her that she was there to attend the same hearing. Her name was Chrisandria Moses, Miashah's mother. The two small victims who perished in a cooking fire on November 18, 2013, at London Square Apartments, a low-income housing project in mid-town Tulsa, were her granddaughters.

She had a gracious persona that belied the warrior beneath, toughened from domestic violence, hardship, and racial disparity tolerated for decades in Tulsa. Through years of struggle she had worked her way from menial tasks to higher positions that commanded a measure of respect, a security guard, a licensed nursing assistant, and, until recently, a Tulsa public school bus driver. She was a passionate, well-spoken, God-fearing woman who knew common sense from nonsense, which is exactly what she believed the justice system had perpetrated on her daughter.

I had no connection to the case other than a long-standing friendship with the bail bondsman, Dennis Wharton, who had mentioned to me that the Moses family had only limited means. Sharon Holmes, their pro-bono attorney, told Wharton the family was struggling to pay Miashah's out-of-pocket legal costs for documents and transcripts needed to defend her. She told Wharton she felt the District Attorney's (DA) stance in the case was harsh and unwarranted. Wharton gave her $500 to help the family with legal expenses.

I had never met Holmes, but Wharton knew her well, along with many judges and attorneys in the Tulsa district criminal courts. He had been a bail bondsman for 18 years and was a licensed California attorney. "I don't think the facts support the charges," Wharton confided to me.

Local news outlets adopted a different view from Wharton's. Given skeleton facts from police and fire reports, television networks dispensed graphic footage of the inferno. They vilified Miashah with a sullen mug shot, noting that she locked the doors and left the girls "trapped" inside to die. [2 3]

In the ensuing weeks, I found myself driving through the area, peering up at apartment buildings for a fire-damaged roof. When I turned toward London Square Apartments, I saw the visible scar—scorched wood siding spreading upward from the second-floor balcony to the peak of the roof, a frightening marker of two dead children.

Suddenly, the dynamics of the case—the fire, the media coverage, Wharton's support—became very real to me.

Thus, my attendance at the hearing that day, and then many more.

The Moses family's presence was huge, supportive, and dedicated, something I witnessed first-hand when I stepped off the fourth-floor elevator and encountered a large group of relatives carrying large posters with photos of the two small fire victims.

More than a dozen Moses family members of all ages were joined together, from Miashah's sister Nubia, a 13-year-old honor student, to Doreen, the children's grandmother, torn between the desperate loss of her little ones and the empty answers as to why.

Perhaps the most important family member was Keahmiee, the children's 19-year old mother, who had come to defend her sister's innocence even through the pain of her own devastating loss. "Nobody asked me," she said. "I'm their mother, and I'm telling you my sister is not a murderer. My sister loved my kids."

The outpouring was an odd combination of rejoicing, remembrance, and a hard-core defense of a family member whom they believed was nothing more than another victim of the accident herself. It was a family at once torn apart and held together by the same twisted act of fate.

I was struck by Chrisandria's grit and determination as we sat on the bench that morning. This effervescent black woman was a mix of grace and brutal frankness. No one had to wonder what was on her mind. Courtney Fletcher, her soul mate of 17 years, shook my hand and introduced himself, the epitome of a soft-spoken gentleman.

I was raised in a middle-income white family in Tulsa and was generally oblivious to racial issues of the time. That is, until I wandered through the fallen shambles of the old Tulsa downtown train station whose operation had been, quite literally, stopped in its tracks. Rail cars were left standing frozen in time. The tracks that sliced a clean line between Tulsa's north side black community and south side white community had long since been left rusted and abandoned. Wandering through the old station, I was perplexed by a solid granite placard over a water fountain inscribed, "Whites Only."

My mother would later recount a bit of personal history that lent relevance to the rubble. Our city had the unfortunate distinction of hosting the 1921 Tulsa Race Massacre, one of the largest slaughters of African Americans in U.S. history, an event that left Greenwood, a thriving north Tulsa black community known as Black Wall Street, burned to the ground. She said my grandfather was an early member of the Ku Klux Klan in Tulsa, one of the first Klan groups to aggressively recruit male activists. He was there with his shotgun alongside other Klan members that infamous day in 1921—a family fact that lifted the violence and prejudice from the pages of history and dropped it squarely in my own backyard.

And while the tragedy is largely forgotten almost 100 years later, the embers of that event still burn silently through the ranks of law enforcement, the court system, and everyday conversations in the streets of Tulsa.

This was my first encounter with the other side of the tracks, the part of our community that lives a very different life from my own and with vastly different challenges.

Transitioning this ingrained, bifurcated perception into an equitable perspective takes more than words. It takes action. It takes involvement. It takes exposure to life as black people have lived it for generations.

Which is what I inadvertently got.

Gathered around were sons and daughters, mothers, grand-mothers, uncles, aunts, and friends, all immediately as open as a book. No prissy-hidden proper agendas or polite plastic words. Somewhere in that brief experience, I entered a fresh new world.

In the days and weeks that followed, I became engrossed in the overwhelming dilemma they faced. The sadness, anger, and futility of facing down an overbearing District Attorney and court system with unlimited resources and unrestrained power pitted the Moses family in an uphill battle for justice.

Immersing myself in this case convinced me there is an untold side of the story, vastly different than the versions law enforcement and the justice system spoon-feed to the public.

To say there is no racism today is delusional. You can say you've never experienced it or seen it, but that doesn't change the reality that racism is alive and well. I was lulled into believing this myself until I was standing in the midst of the ugly reality.

We see it in the vast number of minority and low-income people across the country unjustly incarcerated at the hands of a flawed justice system and aggressive law enforcement officers—shielded by the law—whose actions persist in crowding our jails and prisons with those who have little knowledge, access, or means of defending themselves. Unfortunately, my home state is the epitome of that retribution. Oklahoma has led the nation in the incarceration of women since 1991.

Lest I forget to mention it, I was told that my grandfather came home that night in 1921 and put his shotgun away in the closet. He told my mother he wanted no part of what he saw. The next day, he resigned from the Ku Klux Klan. His revulsion is ingrained in my DNA.

*

Introduction

The mass incarceration of women

THE ugly truth has been there for years.

In 2016, Oklahoma became the largest per-capita incarcerator on the planet.[4] Even more alarming, as of 2019 the state has led the nation in putting women behind bars for more than 30 years, a disproportionate number of them women of color.[5]

Prisons are barren, frightening places that house the good, the bad, and the innocent together in one large bowl of prison soup, subjecting them to subhuman conditions while denying them basic constitutional rights.

That's where we warehouse women who have hit rock bottom, women for whom we have no other place. The slightest infraction, with little or no evidence, can land a woman behind bars for decades, possibly the rest of her life, deprived of the oxygen of freedom.

The burden of the state's high incarceration rate falls hardest on women of color. Black women are incarcerated at about twice the rate of their representation in the state's adult population. The truth is that in too many states black women are denied the same justice afforded white women. Even black men don't suffer the same consequences as their female counterparts.[6]

Unseen, confinement is where society's unspent rage takes its toll on human lives. It reduces existence to a room that grows smaller with each degradation. A house of pain and trauma, its concrete walls and steel doors enclose people in jails and prisons, juvenile facilities, solitary, immigration detention, and civil commitment. Incarceration intersects punishment, dignity, and end of life. And fear of its horrors are the bludgeon of interrogations, plea bargaining, and retributive justice.

Dehumanization spreads through imprisonment like a virus, eroding human life by indifference to suffering and the perpetuation of violence. Indeed, confinement is where sustenance becomes punishment, neglect substitutes for care, and the mind is wasted and destroyed.

The correctional system hasn't adapted to the large increase in incarcerated women.

Women are jailed simply because they can't make bail for minor offenses or can't attend a court appearance because they can't find a babysitter, miss work, or lack transportation. Women wind up in the state's prison system, where they are stripped of moral autonomy and denied the benefit of every doubt, the simple dignity of being believed, and the capacity for suffering.

Hence, prison is where myths and stereotypes hold sway, fed by social biases and prejudices, demolishing the notion that the punished can also be victims. Punishment, more so than conviction, denotes the character of inmates, often causing their prison guards to see abuse as justified and to discard the idea that inmates could be victims of mistreatment. So, in dark corridors where there is no moral restraint, no accountability, no limit to harm, retribution is doled out, often by overbearing, underpaid guards with cold-hearted ways of giving and getting what they want.

Women can be shackled during childbirth. They can be placed in solitary confinement. They can have their complaints of contractions, bleeding, and labor ignored and deliver babies in jail cells or prison cells. They can be denied their right to access abortion. They can be denied access to quality prenatal care.

The consequences for children born to an incarcerated mother—or of having an incarcerated parent—are profound later in life, especially when we consider the deep racial disparities in incarceration rates. Thus, the cycle of incarceration continues as generations of low-income minorities are whiplashed into the prison system with little means of defending themselves.

Jails are facilities for coercing women into plea bargains, for providing business for bail bondsmen, and for punishing women who haven't had a trial and are presumed innocent.

Many arrests result in felony charges, which remain on the offender's record permanently and result in lost job opportunities, low-income wages, and often unaffordable childcare costs for women struggling to regain a foothold in society. Living conditions worsen and basic needs go unmet. Children suffer.

Nowhere is this problem starker than in Oklahoma, where eighty-five per cent of incarcerated women are mothers.[7] [8]

Nearly forty per cent of women in prison have been physically or sexually abused,[9] a fact underscored in Oklahoma where the prevalence of rape and physical violence toward women by an intimate partner is greater than any other state.[10]

In Oklahoma, a state notorious for locking up more women per capita than anywhere else on Earth, Mabel Bassett, the state's sole medium-maximum security prison, has its own special notoriety.

The 1,200+ inmate facility topped the list for sexual violence in female institutions in the country.[11] In 2014, a Bureau of Justice Statistics survey found that over 15 percent of the inmates surveyed at Mabel Bassett reported some form of sexual abuse or rape from a prison guard or another inmate, double the national average.[12]

Women claimed that surveillance cameras in parts of the facility "were either not properly installed in that area or were kept in [an] ongoing state of disrepair," and that prison guards took advantage of this security lapse.[13]

In July 2013, eleven women serving time in Oklahoma prisons filed a federal lawsuit claiming they were sexually assaulted by three guards at Mabel Bassett Correctional Center. According to federal court documents, the wardens created "a corruptive den for sexual depravity" where the guards were authorized to prey upon and commit acts of excessive force against inmates whenever and wherever they chose without meaningful consequences. Oklahoma state prison officials refused to testify at the hearing.[14] [15]

"We send people to prison and we punish them for what they've done," said Pottawatomie/Lincoln County District Attorney Richard Smothermon, who prosecuted the case against Mabel Bassett. "But that should not include being victimized, raped, abused by other people behind bars or prison guards." [16]

Women are the fastest-growing correctional population in the country. And beyond the headlines, beyond the statistics, beyond the prevalent notion that these women are where they belong, the result isn't pretty.

You don't know what it's like until you creep up to the edge of the swamp and peer into its fetid core.

*

Prologue
The massacre

THE 1921 Tulsa Race Massacre is something most Oklahoma citizens would rather forget.

The horror of the holocaust that left Tulsa's affluent black district burned to the ground is revealed only in the tattered letters, faded postcards, and grainy photos left behind by those who witnessed it. Now, a century later, the lurid details are coming to light—as they did at the first light of dawn for Eldoris McCondichie on the morning of June 1, 1921.

"Get up! Get up!" Eldoris' mother's scream pierced the early morning air. "The white people are killing the colored folks!" Surely it was a bad dream. She was only nine.[17]

It was still dark when the family began to stir. Outside they could hear explosions, tramping footsteps, and the rattle of a wagon bumping down the street with a machine gun mounted on the back. Black men, women, and children were running. Some were heading for the railroad tracks, hoping for safety on the other side, only to be shot dead between the rails.

The Frisco railroad tracks, known as "The Line," was the demarcation down Tulsa's Greenwood district that separated the marginalized black families on the north side from their affluent white counterparts on the south side. The black families were desperately trying to reach the south side to escape a hail of gunfire, torches, and turpentine bombs heaved from small airplanes buzzing overhead like viperous insects.[18]

Eldoris barely had time to throw on a dress and grab her shoes and socks before her father yanked her out the front door.

The family watched speechless, struck mute, almost paralyzed by the otherworldly spectacle unfolding around them. A cloud of smoke became more intense. A Greenwood man ran across the alley and was cut down by a shotgun blast. Black people by the hundreds were running down the railroad tracks, running and running, desperately trying to escape the horrors of the riot. Women and children were running, some women still in their nightgowns holding their crying children's hands and dragging them along.[19]

Others in Greenwood were awakening to the horrific scene unfolding around them. Dr. Andrew Jackson, a successful young black doctor, stepped out of his office door to see roofs of buildings, churches, schools, a hospital, exploding in flames. Flaming turpentine balls were falling on the steps in front of him.

The holocaust began on May 31, 1921. Those who survived would never forget its intensity. But Dr. Jackson never got a chance to remember. Bullets tore into him before he could make it to nearby Standpipe Hill, a landmark in the Greenwood district that had been taken over by an angry mob of vengeful whites.

John Oliphant, a prominent white 73-year-old retired judge, had built a fancy home near the top of Standpipe Hill several years before other black families began to build equally fancy homes. Dr. Jackson was his doctor and a trusted friend. Oliphant woke up that morning to see soldiers from the National Guard and veterans in khaki uniforms lined up along the crest of Sandpipe Hill just south of his home. They fired east toward the black gunmen holed up in the belfry of Mount Zion Baptist Church and inside a nearby high school. [20]

"We're going to make the destruction complete," one of the men bragged.

Dr. Jackson picked up his bag and rounded the corner of his house, nodding to Oliphant who lived just a few doors down. Seven or eight men with rifles were milling about, some dressed in khaki uniforms, some in civilian clothes.

"Here am I," Jackson said to them. "Take me."

Two of the boys raised their rifles.

"Don't shoot him!" Oliphant yelled. "That's Dr. Jackson."

But one of the boys didn't listen. He fired two shots into Jackson's chest. When the doctor fell, the second boy stood above him and fired another shot into Jackson's leg. [21]

As the white marauders moved north on June 1, they put a torch to more than 1,115 black homes, five hotels, 31 restaurants, 24 grocery stores, the black hospital, the public library, and a dozen churches, including the community's most magnificent new edifice, Mount Zion Baptist Church dedicated only two months earlier. The smell of death floated through the streets like a summer fog.

By June 2, 1921, 6,000 Greenwood residents were in custody, having been moved from detainment in McNulty Park and the Convention Hall into pig and cow barns at the Tulsa County Fairgrounds. This gave white gangs the time that they needed to destroy Greenwood, to loot, pillage, and burn. White women and children began to appear among the looters of black homes about the time the National Guard appeared.

Two-slatted cattle trucks inched by in succession, bodies stacked haphazardly, as if whoever put them there was in a hurry. Black arms and legs bounced through the slats with each bump on the road. A dead woman's legs dangled from the open tailgate of the front truck. Some of the bodies were naked. There were dead children on the trucks, too. A young black boy lay spread-eagle atop the pile of dead on the second truck, dressed neatly as if he had been getting ready for school when the end came.[22] The truck bumped over a pothole and the boy's head rolled. His face showed abject terror as if he had literally been frightened to death. Beside him was an old man with half his skull blown off. These men who had yesterday been fathers, brothers, and husbands protecting their own, were now rotting in the sun.[23]

Eyewitnesses saw black bodies laid out on the banks of the Arkansas River, some of the bodies dumped into the river itself. Others saw bodies tossed into a west Tulsa town incinerator or dumped in mass graves from the backs of flatbed trucks, their bodies tumbling like rag dolls into the trench.[24]

The Stanley-McCune funeral home noted that some of the black bodies were riddled with bullet holes or stabbing wounds. Some had been bludgeoned to death with bricks, bars, or whatever other blunt objects the marauders could get their hands on.

When it was over, Greenwood looked like a war zone. Thirty-five square blocks of the black community lay in ruin.

The day before, Greenwood was the utopia of an aspiring, well-to-do African American community that had defied the odds in 1921

America. Years before, white supremacists in Tulsa had relegated black families to the north side of town, calling it "Little Africa," to keep them poor.

It wasn't simple hate that motivated so many to destroy Greenwood. The destruction and murder were driven by jealousy and white supremacy. Greenwood was thriving, alive with doctors, lawyers, teachers, and preachers. Prominent black people in Greenwood achieved a level of economic success and self-determination that had never existed before for black Americans in the United States, then less than 60 years removed from slavery.

Previously a listless city of 18,000 souls, a dead and hopeless outlook ahead, Tulsa became Oklahoma's most vital boomtown when oil was discovered in 1901. The oil rush created instant wealth for many white people, but also for some of the landowning black people with ties to Native tribes who inherited the land.

After statehood, the first bill proposed by the Oklahoma Legislature was Senate Bill One, which initiated the state to the Jim Crow era and subjected Oklahomans to racial segregation and the black community to oppression.

Segregation forced black people into the north side of the Frisco railroad tracks, and the need for community there created economic opportunity. When the district's first grocery store opened in 1905 at the corner of Greenwood and Archer Street—Black Wall Street was born.[25]

But white people in south Tulsa called it "niggertown." Resentment brewed among white people about the rising wealth and confidence of black Americans, not only in Oklahoma but across the United States. Ku Lux Klan membership, fueled by disgruntled Civil

War Confederates still embittered by the freed black slaves, had been growing rapidly in boomtown Tulsa.

By 1921, Greenwood had a high school that taught Latin, chemistry, and physics, a three-story hotel with a chandeliered living room, and a silent movie theater accompanied by a live pianist. Greenwood's most successful entrepreneurs reinvested in the community, building parks and additional housing. Elegant homes lined its most prominent residential avenues.

This caused a bitter resentment on the part of the lower order of whites, who felt that the colored men, members of an "inferior race," were exceedingly presumptuous in achieving greater economic prosperity than they who were members of a divine order superior race. [26]

But in Tulsa, nothing inflamed white people more than what they saw across the railroad tracks in Greenwood—the sturdy, brown-brick businesses along Greenwood Avenue, the fancy homes, the cars, and the gold pieces flashed around even by shoe shiners. There was a basic lack of respect for black people; their status as second-class citizens in the state was accepted by virtually all white folks as "the natural order of things." In the hierarchy of dark-skinned sins, "uppityness" was second only to defiling white women.

Which is what started it all on that otherwise placid Memorial Day afternoon in 1921.

On May 30, Dick Rowland, a 19-year-old black shoe shiner known as "Diamond Dick" was working in a whites-only parlor in the Drexel Building on Main Street in downtown Tulsa. Since there were no restrooms for black people in the facility, an arrangement was made for people of color to use the restroom on the top floor. The elevator operator was Sarah Page, a 17-year-old white woman. No one knows exactly what took place in the elevator. Some say the two had a love affair, while others believe Rowland tripped walking into the elevator. In some way, Rowland touched Sarah. By the time the elevator doors reopened, Page was screaming and Rowland was running for his life.

The elevator incident soon became a "full-fledged sexual assault" in the eyes of some whites. A rumor of rape was spread further by a *Tulsa Tribune* article the next day that claimed that Rowland had tried to tear off Page's clothes. The news story ran with the headline "Nab Negro for Attacking Girl in Elevator" along with an ominous editorial: "To Lynch Negro Tonight."

Rowland was arrested and locked in the local city jail, where black Tulsa residents feared he might be dragged out and lynched for his alleged crime.

Without pausing to ascertain whether or not the story was true, a mob of embittered whites incited by the Klan were deputized and set forth on a wild rampage. Eventually, their numbers grew to the thousands. Rowland was quickly moved six blocks from the ramshackle city lockup to the country jail on the sixth floor of the courthouse, where the sheriff disabled the elevator fearing that a lynching was about to take place. [27]

About 9 o'clock p.m. on May 31st, guards reported that a crowd of white men were gathering near the courthouse and that threats of lynching a negro were being made and negroes in "Little Africa" were arming to prevent it. A small entourage of black men, some of them armed, drove downtown on the evening of May 31 to ensure that Rowland was safe. They found a crowd of hundreds of white men, many of them also armed, outside the courthouse.

Eventually, a black World War I veteran and a white man got into a scuffle over the veteran's right to wield a weapon. A gunshot rang out, and within minutes Tulsa was at war.

As many as 5,000 armed whites, hundreds of them deputized by the police, descended on Greenwood that night and into the next morning, using a mixture of plundering, coercion, and violence to reassert the racial hierarchy they desired for Tulsa.

The ones who didn't have weapons soon acquired them. A uniformed police officer shouted, "Get a gun and get a nigger!" And they did.[28]

For two days beginning on May 31, 1921, the mob set fire to hundreds of black-owned businesses and homes in Greenwood. More than 300 black people were killed. More than 10,000 black people were left homeless, and Black Wall Street was left smoldering.

Houses were looted for their valuables, like jewelry, as well as precious memorabilia, like family Bibles. Grand pianos and fine Victorian furnishings were towed or carried out of homes. If the invaders found a home still occupied, they'd sometimes lead residents to a detention center in downtown Tulsa. Other times, they'd murder the occupants.[29]

Ten Greenwood men firing from the Mount Zion Baptist Church tower never made it out. They died in a hail of gunfire from Standpipe Hill. White men emptied their guns into the bodies of the black men, then kicked the corpses when their guns were empty.

Hell itself could not have been worse.

Survivors talk of how the city was shut down during the riot. The phone systems and the railways were cut, and the Red Cross wasn't allowed in. Postcards taken during the massacre show burning corpses.

"They tried to kill all the black folks they could see," a survivor said. "They took everything they thought was valuable. They smashed everything they couldn't take."

There was complicity between the city government, the police, and the mob, and after two nightmarish days in 1921, one of the worst episodes of racial violence in American history left Black Wall Street burned to the ground.

For years black women would see white women walking down the street in their jewelry and snatch it off.[30]

Greenwood aftermath of 1921 Tulsa Race Massacre

(Courtesy/Special Collecti0ns/McFarlin Library/The University of Tulsa)

The charges against Dick Rowland were eventually dropped. Sarah Page gave a statement to police recanting her assault claim just hours before the shooting started. Rumors said they both moved to Kansas City. In the end, an all-white jury attributed the riot to the black mobs, while noting that law enforcement had failed in preventing the riot.

Tulsans refused to speak of that bloody chapter for decades, keeping it out of history books and personal family histories. Not a single white person was ever charged with a crime. Black people, facing an uncertain path forward in Greenwood, lived in tents on the plots of their former houses. Though the attack initially prompted a wave of outraged articles, it quickly receded from the collective memory.[31]

Tulsa has been in denial over the fact that people were cruel enough to machine-gun black families in the streets and bomb them from the air. The violence that destroyed Greenwood and the conditions that led to it are legacies many would rather forget. But Eldoris remembered. Seventy-nine years later, she was one of the few survivors who lived to recount the story.

There's horror in the history of Greenwood. Nearly a century later, the horror still runs silently through the streets of Tulsa and the halls of the Oklahoma judicial system. The nooses have long since left the trees, but their specters hang like ghosts in the halls of justice.

They've stopped lynching blacks in Oklahoma, but they haven't stopped persecuting them.

PART 1

TRIAL BY FIRE

She left to throw a dirty diaper in the trash.
Then everything changed.

1

Unit #716

IT was a joke among maintenance workers in the run-down apartment complex: "Black people frying chicken with grease, they keep burning down these apartments!" The rag-tag maintenance crew at the Section 8 housing project found it a convenient answer for local fire marshals who never bothered to investigate further.

The aging London Square Apartment complex was a misfit in the midst of a well-established south Tulsa neighborhood in central Oklahoma. When it was built in 1965, the sprawling complex was considered a jewel in the midtown community, boasting seven private in-ground swimming pools and immaculate landscaping. Now, 50 years later, local neighbors saw it as a tinderbox, its aging wood roofs, dilapidated stairs, and boarded windows all testaments to neglect and the relentless march of time. Numerous cooking fires through the years served only to evacuate the unlucky tenants and the colonies of bed bugs hiding in the mattresses of the burned-out units. Nearby residents in well-manicured homes hoped for its condemnation by city officials, but it never came. Only more fires.

One of those occurred on November 18, 2013.

The nightmare began with a plume of black smoke. Miashah Moses saw it rising from her building as she crossed the parking lot of London Square Apartments. Panicked, she broke into a run. Her two small nieces were inside the apartment.

She raced up the staircase to her front door, still unsure if the smoke was coming from her unit. She was shaking so badly she kept dropping her keys. Frantic, she ran next door to #718 and pounded on Tina Long's window, screaming, "Fire! Call 911!" Tina dialed 911 and bolted out her door down the walkway to Miashah's apartment. Neither could budge the door. Noni, 4, and Nylah, 18 months, were trapped inside. They were the children of Miashah's younger sister, Keahmiee Moses.

Miashah, a 23-year-old African American, had only recently moved into unit #716 on the second floor of the complex and had left the apartment only a few minutes earlier to empty the trash.

Two men appeared out of nowhere and tried futilely to bust the door open. Finally, on Tina's count, they rammed the door off its hinges. A wall of thick black smoke rolled out, and the two men lunged in, only to be driven back coughing and spewing smoke. They couldn't see two inches in front of their faces. They tried to enter again and again, but each time were forced back by the smoke.

Tina wasn't giving up. "I had on a really thin T-shirt, and I bunched it up as best I could over my face and I made it to the hallway. I couldn't breathe anymore. And I started thinking of my kids and I thought, 'I can't die here, I've got kids.'" She turned and retreated.

Visibility was near zero and the heat level was approaching that of spontaneous ignition. Miashah knew where the children were and was determined to save them or die trying. She nearly did die. After several attempts to grope her way along the hallway to the bedrooms, she collapsed outside from smoke inhalation.

By this time, temperatures in the ultra-dense smoke had reached flashover. Within seconds, fifteen-foot flames were leaping out the kitchen window. "She would have gone in again had one of the guys not physically restrained her," Tina said, "and she would have been dead along with the children."

"I didn't hear smoke detectors going off anywhere," Tina said. "All I could hear was Miashah screaming, 'My babies, my babies, get the babies!'"

Tina was kneeling over a smoke victim in the courtyard below when she caught a glimpse of the apartment maintenance worker running up the stairs, across the second-floor walkway, and throwing something that looked like a smoke detector into the burning unit. "I can't be sure, but it was round and white and looked just like the smoke detector in my unit," she said. "I mean, what else would he be throwing in there?"[32]

Fire trucks arrived within minutes, and firefighters struggled to drag the hose from the hydrant across the street some 300 feet around the full length of the building, up the back stairs, and across the walkway to #716. Several fire hydrants inside the complex had stopped working several years ago and were plugged. "I felt like it was taking forever," Tina said. "It was probably 10 or 15 minutes just to get the hose up."

After Miashah's frantic call, Courtney Fletcher, her stepfather, rushed to the scene and found her on the sidewalk in the midst of firefighters, hoses, and a plethora of tenants and onlookers. Her screams of "Save my babies!" were lost in the surrounding chaos.

By this time smoke was belching from the balcony of #716 across the entire complex the length of a football field. Fire Captain Zachary Willis was parked on the side of the complex in a city SUV talking to a fireman in Engine 9 when Courtney approached his window.

"They were just standing there like nothing serious was happening," said Courtney. "There're two kids in that corner unit!'" he shouted, pointing to #716.

Willis appeared to be caught off guard. "At this point I was still unaware of possible victims inside the apartment," his report states. "I had the captain from Engine 14 at the window of the car when a friend of the mother approached us stating there were kids inside the apartment." Another fire unit had become aware and tried to radio out but was "stepped on" by another radio call.

The frightened children were just inside the window, but Fire Captain Stan May said firefighters didn't know this and came in from the other side.[33]

Tina watched helplessly as firefighters emerged carrying the small limp bodies to a waiting ambulance. The girls were rushed two miles to the St. Francis Hospital emergency room.

News of the children's death came in the harshest way. Members of the Moses family were crowded in the hospital emergency waiting room praying the girls would pull through when a uniformed stranger approached and asked the names of the children "for the coroner."

They stared in disbelief.

2

Life in Section 8

MIASHAH and her younger sister, Keahmiee, 19, moved to London Square only two months before the fire. Miashah worked mornings at the Tulsa Transit Station, and Keahmiee worked afternoons as a housekeeper at Hillcrest Hospital. When Keahmiee worked, Miashah cared for Noni and Nylah, who by all accounts were crazy about their "Auntie Moe."

The cramped two-bedroom apartment where the sisters lived together was Section 8 housing, subsidized housing for low-income families who live below the poverty line as Miashah, Keahmiee, and the two children did. It wasn't the Hilton, but the aging housing complex was affordable and located in a decent part of town near the scenic midtown area. Miashah and Keahmiee were close and glad finally to be out from under their parents' roof.

Keahmiee was a petite girl with smooth, shoulder-length hair and the winsome face of a kewpie doll. Miashah was the opposite: five-foot-two, stocky, and soft-spoken with the boyish appearance of a 12-year-old, which was roughly her age when she began caring for the family babies. Between her six siblings and the extended family, there was always a baby in the house. Miashah was the one who cared for them, juggling homework and diaper changes, then jumping out of bed the next morning to make the opening bell at McKinley Elementary School. She was already making meatloaf at the age of seven.

Feeding and caring for Moses family babies became a way of life for Miashah. She babysat family children all through high school, which eventually included Keahmiee's two children. An unwed mother at 15, Keahmiee was ill-prepared to manage a young child and, as usual, her big sister stepped in to help as she had always done. Miashah had cared for Noni and Nylah since the day they were born. It was a role she came to relish.

Photos of her at her high school graduation show a bright-eyed, exuberant girl in a cap and gown, laughing and waving to onlookers. All she wanted to do was get a job and live her life with joy. Always a tomboy, she loved shooting hoops in the driveway with her younger brother. Family gatherings at the Moses house were jubilant, with smiling Miashah outgoing and talkative, a bright light at the center of things.

Miashah Moses 2009 High School Graduation (Photo: Tulsa Public Schools)

When Keahmiee leased the London Square apartment, it seemed only natural that Miashah would move in with her and help take care of the kids. "That's all I knew, was those kids," Miashah said. "I had been taking care of them my whole life."

The apartment complex occupied a square block and consisted of seven two-story buildings numbered from 100 to 700, each with 20 to 30 apartments housing families of a variety of ages and ethnicities. The sisters occupied a corner unit on the second floor of building 700 directly across from the entrance and vending machines. Their large second-story balcony overlooked a quiet, tree-lined neighborhood street, offering a breath of fresh air on quiet nights.

But certain things about apartment #716 were amiss. Of particular concern was the wooden railing along the second-floor walkway just outside their door, which was missing several slats. Noni was prone to let her little sister out for a walk, and there was ample room for a toddler to squeeze through and plummet to the sidewalk below. Since Noni was able to reach and unlock the door from the inside, Keahmiee and Miashah were careful to lock the dead bolt with their keys from the outside when leaving the apartment, even for a few minutes.

London Square missing slats outside Miashah's apartment (Photo: Carol Mersch)

Also, the dials on the electric stove didn't align with heat levels, and you could never be certain if a burner was on or off. The sisters learned that the only way to turn a burner off was to twist the knob to the right until it stopped, something their neighbor, Tina, was keenly aware of since her stove dials had no heat level markers at all. "They had all worn off," she said. "There's supposed to be a light that turns on when the burner's on, but there's been times when the light's not on, but I know the burner is on because I feel the heat coming off."[34]

There were other issues. The apartment didn't have a smoke detector, and the fire extinguisher outside on the walkway had an expired inspection sticker. Exposed wiring could be seen sprawled along the upstairs walkway and dangling from exterior walls.

Tina worried that the wiring in the aging complex was antiquated and overloaded. The lights in her ceiling fan flickered and wouldn't work at the same time as the fan. Finally, the entire fixture blew. The light in the bathroom short-circuited one day and threw the breaker. Then, when she plugged in a nearby oscillating fan, it sparked and blew the circuits in all three bedrooms. She hesitated to call the supervisor, since, she said, if tenants complained too much about problems, they were threatened with eviction.[35]

Jon Hodges and his girlfriend, Andrea, lived in the apartment below Miashah and had electrical problems of their own. "We had to have our entire apartment rewired because we had several electrical fires," Hodges said. "Like we would be watching TV and all of the sudden the TV would go out and we would see smoke coming out of the wall. There was one time we could actually see a black line starting to burn up the side of the wall." At that point, he threw all the breakers and called the manager.[36]

Nekesha Richards had recently leased an upstairs apartment in building 300. Her stove dials all had heat level markers, but the burners didn't always turn off when she turned the dial to the "off" mark. An exposed lightbulb and its wiring could be seen hanging from the vent hood next to the grease trap directly over the burners. A single mother with two young daughters, a 4-year-old and a 1-month-old, she was frustrated with other issues in the apartment, such as a recurring infestation of bed bugs in her unit that she couldn't seem to get rid of—a problem shared by another tenant across the way in building 700 whose child was often covered with bed bug bites.

While conditions in London Square weren't perfect, Miashah and Keahmiee had never lived outside their home before, so they really didn't know what to expect.

Keahmiee with Nylah and Noni, 2013

3

Not an ordinary day

ON November 18, 2013, Keahmiee fixed herself shrimp in a skillet with grease for lunch and left the skillet on the back burner of the stove. She kissed the children goodbye and left for her two o'clock shift.

Less than an hour later, Miashah heated pre-grilled chicken strips for the children's lunch, a task that took less than five minutes. After feeding Noni, she changed the baby's diaper and put the two girls in her bedroom to watch television. She turned the burner off and left to carry the dirty diaper and the rest of the trash to the dumpster, taking care to lock the door behind her to ensure the youngsters couldn't get out to the walkway with the missing wooden slats.

Surveillance cameras show Miashah leaving her apartment in the far southwest corner of the building and proceeding down the outside stairs to the trash bin in the parking lot directly next to the building. After emptying the trash, she stopped at a pop machine and crossed the parking lot to visit briefly with a tenant who waved her down from a nearby building.

When she turned to head back to her apartment, she saw black smoke billowing from the southwest corner of building 700—right where only a few minutes earlier she had left Noni and Nylah secure and happy, watching television in her bedroom.

The rest was a blur.

As fire trucks, EMS, and Tulsa Police screamed into the complex, Miashah fell to the ground screaming "My babies! Somebody save my babies!" A helicopter from a local news station circled overhead, capturing the ferocious blaze and surrounding chaos. A man was seen trying to climb up the outside of the building to the porch but he fell off because the bricks were too hot.

London Square 2005 fire (Courtesy: Tulsa NewsOn6)

Courtney, Miashah's stepfather, was the first to answer her frantic calls and raced to London Square, where he found her curled up on the ground in front of the complex, hysterical and vomiting from smoke inhalation. He watched as a policeman approached Miashah and threatened to restrain her if she didn't calm down. Courtney wrapped his arms around her and held her tight as they watched #716 burn.

There was nothing they could do.

Miashah's mother, Chrisandria, was completing her shift as a Tulsa school bus driver when her cell phone rang. Drivers are prohibited from using cell phones on duty, so she didn't answer. By the sixth or seventh call, a bad feeling came over her. With the phone in her lap she punched the speaker button. What came next would change her life: Courtney was sobbing and screaming something about the babies, Miashah, and a fire.

The conversation was overrun by an urgent call from the school radio dispatcher: "TPS Route 1120, SB21. Please, come in."

"They almost never used my government call sign," she said. Her hand was shaking as she keyed the radio. An emotional dispatcher pleaded, "Chrisandria, sweetheart, please, please call the office!"

News from the dispatcher confirmed the alarming event. Chrisandria returned the bus to the school bus depot, picked up Keahmiee from work, and drove straight to Saint Francis Hospital. When they entered the children's hospital room, Noni appeared to be sleeping peacefully. "Wake up, baby," Chrisandria whispered, patting her cheek. "Wake up."

The children were pronounced dead at 3:45 p.m. Miashah wasn't there when her nieces died. Courtney had left her with a cousin, as by now she was covered head to toe with vomit.

4

The fallout

WHAT happened next is vivid in Chrisandria's mind.

She had been home from the hospital only a few hours when a Department of Human Services (DHS) representative knocked on her door demanding to question Keahmiee about the dead children. This, along with the negative light already being cast on Miashah by newscasters at the scene of the fire and the utter devastation of ten grieving family members inside the house, drove Chrisandria to the edge. Keahmiee herself hadn't stopped crying in the hours since the fire, and now DHS had dispatched a white woman to interrogate her.

"I just blacked out," Chrisandria said. "You turn it around and get off of my porch!" she screamed. "Do you really want to come inside a houseful of crazy screaming niggers?"—she chose her words pointedly. The woman turned and left.

By this time Keahmiee was in dire emotional straights and Chrisandria drove her to Tulsa's St. John's Hospital, where she was sedated and kept overnight.

The next morning, Chrisandria drove Miashah to the hospital so she could see her sister and try in some way to resolve the terrible event, an event that Miashah herself had yet to fully grasp. But she never made it back to Keahmiee's room. "I think reality kind of set in in the waiting room and I lost control," she said. "I was screaming and crying." Chrisandria gathered her up and left.

As they were leaving the hospital, a black SUV with tinted windows raced through the parking lot toward them and screeched to a halt in front of them. In classic "Law & Order" style, several police officers emerged. They said a disruption had been called in from the hospital by the mother, reporting a disturbance between the two sisters.

"That's not true!" said Chrisandria. "I'm the girl's mother, and I *did not* call in a disturbance!" The officers then said Miashah was being arrested for several "failure to pay" warrants for unpaid fines. An internal police memo, however, states that the police were dispatched to the hospital "in reference to an arson suspect being there"—even though federal Alcohol Tobacco and Fired (ATF) fire investigators concluded arson was not suspected as the cause of the fire.[37] Regardless, "They just do what they want to do," Chrisandria said.

Miashah was handcuffed and burst into tears.

Still traumatized by the death of her nieces less than 24 hours earlier, an exhausted and shell-shocked Miashah was taken to the TPD Detective Division where she was read her rights and asked to sign a virtually-blank Miranda form with only her name scribbled at the top that would waive her right to an attorney. "The police told me when they arrested me it was for restitution I owed," she said. So, believing she had no reason for an attorney, she signed the waiver.

She was then interrogated by two detectives and promptly booked into the David L. Moss Criminal Justice Center (commonly referred to as the Tulsa County Jail) on two counts of child neglect.

Chrisandria was now dealing with not only the loss of her two granddaughters, but the slow emotional demise of her entire family.

"I lost four people," she sobbed. "Two granddaughters and two daughters who will never be the same. *People don't understand how hard this is to live with. I can't sleep. I can't eat. I can't do anything.*"

In the days after the fire, Chrisandria searched desperately for something of Noni's and Nylah's to cling to. "I was having such a hard time, and I couldn't find any of Noni's toys or anything around my house. And I said to myself, 'God, please, let me find a shirt, or a sock, or anything.' It was really too soon, but I went to the babies' apartment and they had put up a memorial outside the apartment, and there were all these teddy bears and stuff like that. I bought Noni that doll in 2010, and she named the doll "Sheah" after Miashah. And when I went there that night, right in front was Noni's doll. The only thing on her was soot on the bottom of her feet, where I could tell she had been in the apartment. And it was my 39th birthday."

Chrisandria Moses outside the Tulsa County Jail (David L. Moss Criminal Justice Center) where Miashah was first locked up.

5

A mother like no other

THERE was no doubt that Chrisandria was a fighter. She had seen her share of trouble from an early age.

A mother at 13, she was seven months pregnant with Miashah, her second child, when her husband attacked her with a screwdriver.

It was 1990. They lived together in their north Tulsa apartment. Only moments earlier, their two-year-old son, Keontae, had been playing nearby on the floor of the apartment. As an argument between Chrisandria and her husband grew heated, he turned and unleashed a torrent of anger on the two-year-old, landing a blow across the child's back that sent blood gushing out of his nose. Defiantly, Chrisandria stepped between them to block his fury. He flung her against the closet door.

Clambering for the first thing she could grasp to defend herself, she reached up and tore a clothes rod from the closet and swung it at him with all her might. He jerked it out of her hands and threw it across the room. It wasn't until he was on top of her that she saw the eight-inch screwdriver over her head, lashing at her wildly—first across her chest, then across her back as she turned and hunched to protect her unborn child. Chunks of flesh were punctured out like divots.

With fists flying, the fight continued into the front yard and out into the street. The last punch blacked her out and she fell to the ground. When she came to, she was drenched in blood. A neighbor was standing over her with a shotgun pointed at her husband. "If you hit her again, I'll blow your head off," he said. It was the only thing that saved her life. Twenty-six years later, the pink jagged scars hashed across her dark skin still bear the signs of his rage.

This was the first battle she fought to protect her children, but it wasn't the last. In the aftermath of the London Square fire that engulfed her daughters' apartment in flames, a debate raged about whether it was a tragic accident or a criminal act.

And Chrisandria vowed to fight.

6

The aftermath

FIVE apartments were heavily damaged and 32 individuals were displaced by the fire. Fire Marshalls and ATF investigators swarmed the scene. Questions of how and why the fire started were answered within 24 hours: unattended cooking with grease.

London Square's insurance company moved swiftly to assess the scene. Within a matter of days, #716 was gutted, and all physical traces of the fire or its cause were destroyed. Somewhere along the way, the stove was removed, its whereabouts unknown.

Tulsa fire investigators officially ruled the fire "accidental," since according to fire analysis there was no indication of foul play. Tulsa's DA Tim Harris, however, drew a different conclusion: The deaths of the children were more than an accident—they were depraved, criminal neglect.

From this point, things moved quickly. On November 26, only a week after her arrest, the DA upgraded Miashah's charges from child neglect to two counts of second-degree murder, one for each dead child, citing "an act evincing a depraved mind" when she fixed the children lunch and left them unattended for eight minutes to empty the trash. She had abandoned the children, he alleged, to do something other than merely empty the trash. The specifics would come later.

The charges came on the same day that Noni and Nylah were laid to rest in Crown Hill Cemetery in two unmarked patches of earth. Money was scarce for the Moses family and grave markers would have to wait. Miashah was not present when the children were lowered into the ground; she was in Pod F-18 of the Tulsa County Jail clad in an orange jumpsuit.

Noni and Nylah's cousin, Marvin, a devout light-skinned youth, held a dozen pink balloons tight in his fist and lifted his eyes to the sky with a simple, heartfelt prayer:

"Give us a sense of peace, Heavenly Father, as we release these balloons up into the heavens that they may receive them, for we do not know why this happened to us, but we do know that you are in control. And we ask in the name of Jesus that you continue to show us the way. Help us to be normal and deal with our regular lives. We ask in the name of Jesus that you comfort us and give us the strength to move forward with this tragic situation that has occurred. We give our faith to you, Heavenly Father, as we release these balloons into the sky. We ask in the name of Jesus that you give them to the babies."

A plethora of pink balloons filled the sky and vanished from view, finding their way to other hearts and places where someone might find them later and wonder—and perhaps in some odd way, sense the import of their journey.

Whether the children's death was a tragic accident or a criminal act depends on which version of the story you believe: that of the scribbled, fifteen-line police report, that of the DA's deductive reasoning, or that of several witnesses who were never questioned.

The police report stated that Miashah was "cooking with grease" and referred to the neighbor who had waved her down as a "homie."[38] But Miashah's neighbor, Tina, contradicted this, saying that Miashah told them she was only heating, not frying, the pre-grilled chicken strips and used Pam Cooking Spray, as called for on the package instructions, rather than grease.

John Soules Foods "Fully Cooked Chicken Breast Strips" Ready in Minutes

"I don't know where they got the idea that there was grease," Tina said. "It almost makes it look like she left grease on the fire cooking. But there wasn't any chicken cooking! It just smelt like fire. And if it's grease fire—I've been in a grease fire too—you smell whatever the grease has cooked while it's burning. So, no, I'm sorry..." she shook her head. "If they saw the pan of grease, they might have assumed that's what was going on. I think they just drew some conclusions. And I'm not sure they're correct."

Chrisandria and Courtney were at the girls' apartment only hours before the fire, and Chrisandria remembers seeing a can of Pam on the counter. The fact that the police report used the word "homie"—a black slang term meaning a friend—to describe a neighbor appeared to be a racist reference to Miashah's African American vernacular.

"That didn't surprise me, especially with the police department around here," Tina said. "I mean, not all of them are bad. I've met some really, really good ones. But there's some that just see us, like, 'Oh, you live here, you must be this, well, *this* must be what happened…" She paused. "And it aggravates me. *You're a police officer and you have that kind of power—and you don't care? Because you need to care in that kind of position*!"

Shortly after the fire, she said maintenance workers were quick to stop by late one evening and put heat level markers on her burner dials. "On the burners, they just put the stickers on these right after the fire," she said pointing to the stove burners. The oven dials, however, still had no heat level markers. "I asked them about the oven control and they said, 'Oh its fine.' So, I'm guessing at temperatures here?!"[39]

The fire report was issued within 24-hours and more or less rubber-stamped the police report, listing the cause as a stove fire ignited by cooking oil due to "unattended cooking." Chrisandria wasn't buying it. "Even '48 Hours' doesn't solve crimes that fast." she said.

All official opinions pointed to Miashah as the obvious culprit. Her wanton disregard for the lives of the two helpless little girls became the tantamount conclusion that colored everything that came after: Miashah had left two small children trapped in an apartment to die a horrific death. On top of that, she was black.

A media frenzy ensued. The fatal accident was hammered endlessly on local news channels and across national multi-media platforms. Tulsa news channels broadcast live photos of the fire with scenes of smoke and flames pouring from the apartment with a cadre of fire trucks surrounding the fiery scene from 3:00 p.m. in the afternoon to nearly 11:00 p.m. that night.

The ensuing TV news coverage the next day was damning in its implications. A local CBS news anchor reported that Miashah had left the children "trapped" in the apartment, implying that she had purposely left them to die.[40] A FOX news channel reporter confronted televisions audiences with: "Two children died that day. Somebody has to be held accountable. Who?"[41]

Headlines poured in across iPads and media devices: "London Square Fire, 2 children dead, 3 adults injured" and "Aunt Charged with Murder in Death of Two Children," accompanied by a barrage of incendiary online reader comments. [42] [43] [44] [45] [46] One reader in particular didn't mince words: "As usual, another negro fried chicken fire… Miashah did not step out to take the trash; she stepped out to go ho'in for some crack. Life in the ghetto."

The comment yielded a furious response from the other side: "I know for a fact [she] was not gone longer than 5 minutes frying no damn chicken, period, because yes she is black and knows how long to leave chicken cooking!"

In a string of 16 contentious barbs, one reader flipped the argument the other direction: "What I am pretty much saying is if this were a beautiful 20-year-old white girl you would be outraged by the accusations. As long as you are flaunting the cross, I don't think Jesus would think much of your blatant racist views there, huckleberry, nor your absolute lack of compassion."[47]

It appeared as though every media outlet—print, TV, and online—was showing a grim unflattering mugshot of Miashah with a clenched jaw and close-cut boyish crop.

Chrisandria was mortified.

"I know Miashah. I know my daughters... I have seven children. And I would leave Miashah at home at seven and eight years old because I couldn't afford a babysitter. She would cook *whole meals.* She would never do this, never in a trillion years... We're the ones who lost the babies and they treat us like criminals."

A systemic racial divide was opening wide—one that had burned silently for decades through the ranks of law enforcement, the judicial system, and everyday conversations in the streets of Tulsa, home of the 1921 Tulsa Race Riot, the largest mass-lynching of African Americans in U.S. history that left the affluent Greenwood community known as "Black Wall Street" in ashes.

"I think that we've got really a perfect storm for police shootings in Oklahoma," ACLU of Oklahoma Legal Director Brady Henderson said. "Trust and rapport between law enforcement and many citizens is at an incredible low. The officers start fearing for their safety and so the hands start going closer to the triggers on both sides."[48]

7

The witness

AFTER fading from the headlines for several months, the case erupted again after a March 13, 2014, preliminary hearing when Assistant DA Sarah McAmis purported to have evidence that Miashah had left to do more than just empty the trash—she had gone to another apartment building to buy drugs. The fire that killed the children, she contended, resulted when Miashah willfully left a pan of hot grease heating on the stove to pursue a drug deal with a neighbor.

While the Fire Department's original determination that the fire was "accidental" might have been grounds for child neglect, the fact that the girls' death occurred in conjunction with a crime allowed McAmis to press for a conviction of felony child neglect—defined in Oklahoma criminal code as grounds for second-degree murder.

To do this, McAmis had to prove that not only did Miashah cause the girls' deaths by deliberately locking them in the apartment with a pan of hot grease cooking on the stove, but that she left for the purpose of transacting a drug deal. Emptying the trash, McAmis claimed, was merely something she did on the way to buy drugs.

"Child neglect" in Oklahoma means "the willful or malicious neglect of a child under 18" and is altogether unforgiving, offering prosecutors broad latitude in its application.

McAmis' star witness was Torrance Williams, the co-worker in building 400 who waved Miashah down. Williams, a husky, 20-year-old black man, had previously worked with Miashah at the Tulsa Transit downtown bus station and was visiting his cousin in London Square the day of the fire. McAmis alleged that Williams made a statement to Tulsa police detectives on the scene that Miashah had come to the apartment around the time of the fire and confronted him about a dispute with his cousin over drug money that she owed for marijuana. McAmis contended that Williams specifically told detectives that Miashah was acting, in his words, as if she were high, that she was aggressive, that she was paranoid, and that her eyes were wide.

Tulsa County District Court Judge David Youll was presiding over the preliminary hearing in Miashah's criminal case.

When Williams took the stand, McAmis quickly led him to her point. His answers were not what she expected.

"You formed an opinion that she was under the influence of something, this female. Is that correct?"

"Yes."

"All right. And what led you to form that opinion."

"I mean, 'cause you could tell. Just like it wasn't hard to see that she was drunk off dope. She was drunk off (unintelligible) or (unintelligible)—I mean, like she was just slurring her words. I mean, I know that. But I don't know nothing about buying—about anything like drugs or pills or nothing like that."

"All right. And on that day, did you, in fact, sell her any marijuana?"

"No."

"Did she ever act aggressively towards you that day?"

"No."

"Did she act paranoid towards you that day?"

"No."

"Did you ever tell the detectives that she acted paranoid towards you that day?"

"No."

"And specifically, the photograph that I showed you earlier, State's…"

"No."

"Exhibit 3, did you ever tell the detectives that this was, in fact, the woman in State's Exhibit Number 3 who had come to your apartment that day?"

"See… that's what I'm trying to tell you. They never showed me a picture of nobody. They showed me a picture of me walking to my house. And they said that she came to my house and I told them, yes, a female came to my house that—that had short hair with a tattoo right here. *But that's not her*," he said, pointing to Miashah.

The judge asked, "A tattoo right where?"

"Right here," Williams said, indicating to his lower right eye… And like I told him, how can I come to court about somebody that—that they never showed me?"

From the visitors' gallery, Miashah's older brother, Keontae, let out an audible "Alright!" from the back of the courtroom. Keontae, a lanky 25-year-old, had been especially close to his little sister Miashah since the day she was born and was relieved by Williams's refusal to identify her. The outburst interrupted court proceedings and caused Judge Youll to direct his attention to Keontae at the back of the courtroom.

"Okay, folks, let me explain something to you. If I hear anything from the gallery that's sufficient to disrupt the proceedings, you may be held in direct contempt of court. Direct contempt of court carries up to six months in the Tulsa County Jail and up to a $500 fine. So now that everybody is aware of that. I want to make sure we understand the rules. And likewise, if you leave the courtroom, you're going to stay out."

Judge Youll continued, "I was going to say, Counsel, my understanding is that at some point he alluded to the fact that the female was not *this* female."

McAmis replied, "Yes, Your Honor. Again, the State should have the opportunity to impeach him with prior inconsistent statements," essentially implying that Williams was lying on the stand.

Judge Youll pressed her, "Has he provided any substantive testimony that would assist the Court today? I mean, *you're impeaching your own witness...*"

McAmis, still visibly upset at Torrance Williams' failure, or refusal, to respond as she planned, continued to pursue her interrogation of Williams over repeated objections by Holmes, who believed McAmis intended to defame Miashah.

"...Was your conversation that day between you and the female about drugs?

"No."

"Did you ever tell anyone that it was?"

"No."

"Did you ever tell the detectives that it was about money that the female owed your cousin for drugs?"

"No."

McAmis' questions were redundant to the point of hounding, and Sharon Holmes had reached her limit. She interjected, "Your Honor, I'm going to object to this whole line of questioning. When Mr. Williams first took the stand, he did indicate *that this was not the female*, so we don't know who that is."

McAmis acknowledged the judge's concern, but continued questioning Torrance Williams, painting a vivid picture of Miashah as the drug-crazed woman in question, even though Williams had clearly stated the black woman who came to his building to settle a drug buy with his "big cousin" was not Miashah. A common tactic of prosecutors is to throw enough spaghetti at the wall so that something would stick.

But the spaghetti wasn't sticking with Torrance Williams. His testimony contradicted the DA's basis for charging Miashah with two felony counts of child neglect—specifically, that Miashah locked her nieces in the apartment to buy drugs.

Williams was excused from the stand. McAmis then proceeded to call witnesses from the Tulsa Police and Fire Departments—witnesses she likely hoped would better support the DA's theory.

8

Brick by brick

McCAMIS called Tulsa Fire Department Investigator Mark Milstead to testify. Milstead, a seasoned Fire Marshall with impressive credentials, gave a meandering, detailed, and technical description of the heat levels and path of the fire from its ignition source on the stove burner through the apartment from the ceiling to the floor. However, when McAmis asked if Miashah's statement that she left the stove on low heat was consistent with his own findings, Milstead was unable to give a definitive answer.

"The stove hood had extensive oxidation, which means extensive fire damage to that hood element… We—we are currently going to try to do some investigation and more data to get more of a finite detail… So with that information, you know, it would take, obviously, a lot longer with a low versus a higher temperature to reach that."

He went on to add, "In the hallway, I located a smoke detector that was battery powered that was on the floor between the two bedrooms… It did have a battery located inside it with the numbers 6 of 15, assuming that's the expiration date on the battery. But it was still intact, plugged in; however, it wasn't operational, obviously, at that point."

McAmis asked him to continue. "Okay. Keeping going."

Milstead: I also observed the two bedrooms. We had extensive smoke staining throughout the bedrooms. And smoke staining is just when you have smoke deposit on the wall. Generally, that will start at the upper levels and work its way down. We had smoke staining from floor to ceiling, meaning that, you know, we had a heavy amount of smoke inside that apartment in both bedrooms.

McAmis: And you were mentioning the two bedrooms. And you said you had two civilian victims. Where were the two civilian victims located?

Milstead: Yes. Based on the fire firefighters' statements to myself, one, the older child, was located in the southwest bedroom. She was found in a prone position, which is on her stomach, underneath—partially underneath the bed. She also was covered partially with covers and a pillow. And the younger child was found in the northwest bedroom. And she was located inside the closet doorway of that bedroom, on her back.

McAmis: Okay. And, sir, was it the youngest child in the northwest bedroom that sustained the most injuries?

Milstead: Yes, the child in the northwest bedroom had extensive burn injuries on and about her body... We had fire damage at the upper level, but not at the lower levels. The older child in the southwest bedroom, there were no obvious visible injuries noted on her.

Milstead's testimony that a smoke detector was found in the hallway corroborated Tina Long's statement that she saw the maintenance worker run across the second-floor walkway and throw something into Miashah's doorway. "I know for a fact that's what Eddy threw into her apartment," Tina said. "It was identical to the one in my apartment."[49]

Allen Gorenflo, the last electrician to work in unit #716, knew the layout of the apartment and made a detailed drawing showing that a smoke detector thrown through the front door would have bounced off the inside hall wall of the apartment and landed on the floor between the two bedrooms, precisely where Fire Investigator Milstead said it was found. Gorenflo remembered that the original smoke detector in Miashah's unit was connected to an overloaded circuit that caused a bedroom ceiling fan to malfunction. To relieve the load, the breaker, which was electric and not battery-operated, had been disconnected.[50]

Section 8 housing rules mandate that a functioning smoke detector be installed in each apartment. But Keahmiee and Miashah said there was no smoke detector in the apartment when they moved in. Tina and neighbors who ran to help said they heard no smoke alarms going off.

Milstead, however, was not privy to the situation in the apartment before the fire. His post-fire observations and applied data techniques were derived from his Tulsa Fire Department training and experience. And his knowledge of the children's location and injuries was obtained from a second-hand account, not his own, an account which Chrisandria would later find disturbingly inaccurate.

Milstead was excused from the stand and McAmis called Police Detective Jeanne Mackenzie to the stand. Mackenzie was one of the two detectives who interrogated Miashah immediately after the fire. An attractive blonde who spoke with a slight lisp, she was a nine-year veteran of the Tulsa Police Department and had spent three-and-a-half years as a child crisis detective.

McAmis: "When did your interview take place in relation to when the fire had taken place?"

Mackenzie: "It was the day after the fire."

McAmis: "When you spoke to the Defendant, did you ask what she had been doing before the time of the fire?"

Mackenzie: "Yes. She said that she was cooking on the stove, that she left it on low, that she left the apartment to throw out—to take out the trash."

But when asked again only seconds later, however, Mackenzie contradicted herself, saying Miashah told her she left the stove on "6"—six levels higher than low.

"Did she tell you whether or not she had locked the door to the apartment?" McAmis asked.

"Yes, she said she locked the door because the oldest one would let the youngest one out."

"Did you ask her if she had done anything else outside the apartment other than go to take out the trash?

"Yes, she said that she talked to a gentleman for two or three minutes."

"Okay. Did she tell you, at that point in time she left the apartment, what the two girls were doing?"

"They were in her bedroom, watching TV."

"Did you talk to her about time frames and how long she had been gone?"

"Yes, I asked her when she went to talk to the gentleman, if maybe she was gone more than eight minutes. And her response was 'I hope not.'"

"Did you ask the defendant whether or not she had gone to purchase marijuana from any individual?"

"Yes, I did. She said that was not true."

"Did she make any statements to you about a pop machine?"

"Yes, towards the end of the interview, I asked her about the drink she had in her hand [in the surveillance photo]. She stated that the plan was to go to the dumpster, go to the pop machine, and go back to the apartment. And that's when—she called him Bro—waved her over and she went down to his apartment to talk to him."

"Did she tell you anything else at the fire scene?"

"She stated that she was patted down by somebody from the fire."

Detective Mackenzie's confusion about the heat levels on the stove only added to Chrisandria's belief that the police, as well as the Fire Department, hadn't even a basic understanding of the case they were investigating, and were floundering in preconceived assumptions and shared narratives among the police and fire investigators. She said, "I mean, the main thing is, there is no '6' on the dial! So, I don't know where they get '6' from."

The stove was now gone, likely impounded somewhere in the catacombs of the Fire Department warehouse or deposited in a rusting city trash heap. Retrieving the knobs from the burners to verify heat level markings would be nearly impossible.

After the witness testimonies were concluded, Judge Youll grappled with McAmis' contention that leaving a child unattended for eight minutes would constitute neglect.

"What it gets down to is: Is this a case, then, of child neglect? Reviewing what the definition of child neglect… under which definition of neglect is the State proceeding? Do we know?"

"Yes, Your Honor," McAmis responded. "Under the failure to provide either adequate shelter and/or adequate supervision by leaving these two, a two-year-old and a four-year-old, approximately, alone and unsupervised in an apartment that then caught fire and consumed both of them."

"I mean, is the neglect because it actually caught fire?" the judge persisted. "Are you saying that—at least based on the testimony, the time frame is eight minutes—the fact that the children were left unsupervised for eight minutes is neglect?"

"Yes, Your Honor… Whether or not the time frame really is eight minutes, Your Honor, or whether or not—"

She didn't get any further.

"That's all we have today, right, is eight minutes?" the judge queried. "*Eight minutes being unsupervised is sufficient for child neglect*?"

"Yes, sir."

"So the State could file: one, that the child *was left unsupervised for a minute*, and something happened and then that is sufficient, that would be the State's position?"

At this point, McAmis fell back on the seasoned prosecutor technique of throwing spaghetti at the wall by reciting a vivid cinematic description of events.

"I think it's always fact-dependent, Your Honor. It would determine whether in what condition you left the children. In other words, if you were *cooking in grease* that had been from the night before and you had *it turned it up to '6'* and you left and *dead-bolted the door* and then *went and talked to different people* in the apartment complex, for *whatever length of time*—I do believe that it's always fact-dependent, Your Honor."

Judge Youll nodded to Miashah's attorney, "Ms. Holmes?"

"Your Honor, I would disagree with the State's position. In order to even use child neglect as a predicate for this offense, they'd have to show that the actions taken by Miss Moses were imminently dangerous and also show a depraved mind. Stepping out to empty the trash, we all do it on a daily basis. We don't know whether the fire started two minutes before—two minutes after she walked out or three minutes or five minutes after she walked out. She was conducting an activity that's done in the regular course of everyday business. And I would argue that it's not imminently dangerous to lower the fire on a stove and take the trash out. We go about, again, we go about our business in our homes every day.

Holmes continued: "But my point is, Your Honor, I don't think she carried out any activity that could be considered as negligent. She actually took steps to make sure that nothing happened. She lowered the heat on the stove. She told the detective that she locked the door because sometimes the older child would let the younger child out. It's a horrible situation but in trying to prevent one problem from occurring, this fire cropped up. I think Miss Moses showed that she was very responsible and not negligent."

At this juncture, the judge posed another query to McAmis.

"Would it have been neglect had a fire *not* occurred?"

"It could have been, Your Honor. Depending on the fact circumstances, yes, to leave two children..." she said, doggedly diverting attention away from the fact that Miashah was gone for just a few minutes leading up to the horrible outcome. She argued that it didn't matter how long Miashah was gone, whether it was one minute or eight minutes.

Judge Youll persisted, "No, I understand the facts of this circumstance. What I'm saying, in this particular set of facts, *had a fire not occurred*?"

McAmis maintained her position.

"I believe it could have been, Your Honor. Again, that would be an issue of fact for a jury."

Judge Youll reluctantly yielded to the DA's position. He ordered Miashah held without bond on two counts of second-degree murder and bound over for arraignment by Judge James Caputo in the Criminal Division.

By this time in the hearing, Miashah's brother Keontae had been ushered out of the courtroom by sheriff's deputies and told to leave the courthouse. As he made his way through the foyer, he spotted witness Torrance Williams and stopped briefly to thank him for his testimony. Courtroom deputies were keeping an eye on Keontae and suspected that he was threatening the witness. They told him in no uncertain terms that he was to walk away from the courtroom and leave, which he did. As he proceeded toward the third-floor escalators to leave the courthouse, however, deputies abruptly ordered him to stop, pulled his hands behind his back, and began to handcuff him.

Keontae's aunt, Antonille, was coming up the escalator and was caught off guard. "What's going on?" she asked Keontae. He reached in his pocket and attempted to toss her his car keys, knowing his car on the ground level would be towed if he was booked. As he was trying to explain, deputies ushered him into to an adjacent stairwell and slammed him against a wall, busting his lower lip. He was then escorted into a holding cell in the courthouse, where the arrest report states "a struggle ensued." He was thrown to the floor with enough force to crack his cell phone and dislodge a gold earring. When the gold earring landed on the floor, the deputy smashed it with his foot. The arrest report contains details of the alleged events as reported by the sheriff's deputy:

> I walked Keontae Moses down to the holding cells when he started to fight with us we were taking his property from him to place him in a holding cell. At that time took Keontae Moses to the ground to place leg shackles on him to keep him from kicking us. While on the ground waiting to place leg shackles on him to keep him from kicking us... I removed my Taser and placed it between his shoulders and informed Keontae Moses that if he moved or tried to kick that he would be tased.

Keontae said a struggle never happened. He denied that he ever kicked or fought with the deputies and doesn't recall a Taser stuck in his back or that the deputies really needed one. As evidence of events in the arrest, the report listed "videos found on courthouse cameras located at the Tulsa Courthouse," but when a written request was made for a copy of the videos, the Sheriff's Office responded that they could find "no records responsive to the request."

Chrisandria now had a daughter and a son behind bars.

9

Jailed in the heartland

A half mile north of the courthouse, Miashah was incarcerated in a large windowless concrete structure in downtown Tulsa where visitors are body-scanned for metal objects and weapons. Cell phones and suspicious paraphernalia are seized. Anyone wearing a hoodie is turned away.

When booked into the Tulsa County Jail on November 19, 2013, Miashah joined a cadre of over a thousand women. Oklahoma has the highest rate of female incarceration in the nation—and the world. At the time Miashah was taken to jail, Oklahoma's incarceration rate for women was nearly double the national average, fueled by draconian sentencing laws that hold women longer than men for similar crimes.[51]

Ed Martinez, Jr., a local Hispanic businessman from Tulsa, noted in a 2015 news article that his daughters and other young women frequently describe a common theme when they come into contact with law enforcement:

"Their cell phones are seized, which seems like a personal violation. If they try to prevent this violation, they are threatened with obstruction of justice charges. Women stopped for suspected traffic violations are immediately asked for permission to search their car without probable cause. If they decline, they are threatened with arrest. Once they enter the criminal justice system, they are assessed with multiple fines and fees, most of which support the criminal justice system itself. The state of Oklahoma also enforces sentencing enhancements, mandatory minimums, and harsh drug laws that result in unnecessary felony convictions and long prison sentences for non-violent women."[52]

Multiple charges stemming from a single violation are often piled on by the arresting officer in a practice known as "stacking," where related charges and fines are imposed for essentially the same violation. Many women are unable to pay the steep fines and court costs, and warrants are issued for "failure to pay" and new fines and court costs are added to the old. The system disproportionately harms poor people—and therefore minorities who are disproportionately poor—who often can't afford to miss work, pay for daycare, or find transportation to appear at court hearings and to make payments.

This system, called "policing for profit," feeds on itself, resulting in endless layers of debt for offenders as municipalities and counties attempt to raise revenue on the backs of their most vulnerable citizens to fund administrative costs that often have little to do with judicial procedures, such as law library fees, forensic science improvement fees, trauma care assistance fund, and the information systems revolving fund. Fees and fines make up nearly all of the court system's budget, which means the deputies that arrested Keontae were funded largely by the same low-income people—like Miashah and Keontae—they wield a hammer over.

Unless she were exonerated, Miashah was destined to vanish into the ubiquitous cavern of the living female dead, their hopes and those of their families decimated in the teeth of a merciless legal grinder.

10

Fleeting freedom

NINE months after Miashah's arrest, an ugly comedy of errors ensued when Judge Caputo set Miashah's bond at $60,000. Bail bondsman Dennis Wharton arranged for bail at no charge to the family, and Miashah was, for 24-hours, free. The next evening, however, at the insistence of Assistant DA Steve Kunzweiler, she was ordered back to court for a hearing the next morning at 9:00 a.m.

Her attorney, Sharon Holmes, attempted to reach Chrisandria, Miashah's mother, that night with no luck, as Chrisandria was working the evening shift at a nursing home with no access to her cell phone. Chrisandria was the prime contact for Miashah, since Miashah did not own a cell phone or a car. Though neither Chrisandria nor Miashah had been informed of the hearing, it began as scheduled at 9:00 a.m. the next morning in Judge Caputo's courtroom.

It was in this freak-show nightmare that Miashah's bond began to unravel.

At the hearing, Kunzweiler appeared upset over TV news coverage announcing that Miashah had been released from jail on bond. Judge Caputo, in turn, was upset that Holmes had not advised him of Judge Youll's earlier no-bond ruling. Caputo became further agitated when Miashah failed to appear. Kunzweiler pushed for a total bond of $1 million, $500,000 for each dead child, but Caputo lowered the bond to $250,000 per child for a total of $500,000, and the hearing was adjourned.

Chrisandria finally received Holmes's text message 15 minutes before the 9:00 a.m. hearing was to begin. She and Miashah hurriedly dressed and rushed to the courthouse, arriving around 10:15 a.m., where Miashah was promptly handcuffed and taken back to jail.

Meanwhile, seemingly unaware of Miashah's late arrival, Kunzweiler was standing on the courthouse steps advising news reporters that the defendant's failure to appear proved she "was a flight risk" and "a danger to the community."

It didn't go unnoticed that long-time Tulsa DA Tim Harris was stepping down after 15 years in office and that Kunzweiler was throwing his hat in for the position. His aggressive stance in the case was perceived by some as a move to win public support by projecting himself as a no-holds-barred candidate who was "tough on crime." For those in the north side of Tulsa, this meant that he was tough on blacks.

District Attorney Steve Kunzweiler (Courtesy: Tulsa World)

Chrisandria remembered the State's witness, Torrance Williams, stating during a recess at the preliminary hearing on March 13, 2014, that he was pressured by the DA's office to testify against Miashah in return for leniency on his outstanding drug charge. Tyrone Coleman, Dyanne Coleman, and Timothy Jones were present at the hearing and said they heard the same thing.[53] When Williams refused to implicate Miashah at the preliminary hearing, McAmis threatened to impeach him at the jury trial.[54]

At this point, legal trap doors mysteriously began to open out of nowhere.

Court records show that when Williams appeared on the drug charge five days later, his public defender abruptly resigned. The judge then ordered him to reappear in 30 days with a private attorney. When Williams dutifully reappeared on April 15, but without an attorney, the judge ordered him taken into custody, and he was placed in a holding chair in the courtroom to await booking into the county jail. Somewhere between the holding chair and his actual arrest, however, Williams disappeared from the courtroom. On April 24, 2014 DA Tim Harris issued a bench warrant for his arrest.[55]

But the question of who, if anybody, was responsible for the deaths of Noni and Nylah was more complicated

11

String of fires

THE #716 inferno was only the latest in a long string of fires that had plagued the complex for years. If fire reports were any indication, London Square had become a Virtual incinerator—a scrap pile of outdated wiring, breaker boxes, and patchwork electrical repairs made well before the latest city electrical codes.

But the low-income families in London Square could hardly afford to complain for fear of losing one of the few affordable roofs over their head. Only two months before the #716 fire, a September 2013 fire in building 400 displaced a dozen families when a tenant, Latoya Berry, was frying chicken and witnessed the stove suddenly erupt into flames. "I don't know what happened," Berry said. "I was cooking, it flamed up. I put flour on it. It went everywhere."

In building 500, five people barely escaped their apartment on March 5, 2007, when a bedroom wall inexplicably burst into flames. Inexplicably burst into flames on March 5, 2010. The fire started on the second level of the apartment complex and quickly spread into the attic. Wooden shingles on the roof made controlling the fire difficult. The fire also spread to the basement, where buckets of paint and other cleaning supplies burst into flames. Firemen had to force open several doors and windows to get residents out. At one point, a police officer carried a baby to safety. Sixty people were displaced by the fire. Its cause was listed as "Undetermined."

On February 10, 2007, a fire in building 400 ripped through 27 units. At least 15 families were displaced, and some were left homeless. The fire quickly engulfed a large section of the two-story building from the attic to the basement. Anita Hamblin lived in unit #404 directly beneath the second-story fire and was gone when it broke out. "I ended up moving because [the Tulsa Fire Department] wouldn't let me back in my apartment. Everything I owned was smoke-damaged," she said. Again, the cause of the fire was listed as "Undetermined."

Tulsa Fire Department records show a total of nine building fires in London Square since 2002, although internal accounts reveal other fires since the fire in #716 were handled internally by the maintenance crew and never reported.

Allen Gorenflo, a handyman electrician and long-time resident at London Square, was often called upon to do electrical work. He was among the last to work on #716 prior to its rental to the Moses sisters in 2013. "I lived in the same building. That's the last unit I worked on."

When asked to inspect a dysfunctional ceiling fan in the bedroom of #716, he traced it to a hard-wired smoke detector on the same circuit and said something about the breaker box "didn't look right." He abandoned the project after a London Square maintenance supervisor instructed him to tape electric wires together behind the oven's back wall rather than cap them in a junction box as required by code.

"I may not be a licensed electrician, but I've got 30 years' experience, and I don't do things that way," Gorenflo said.

He recalled another time when London Square asked that he swap out a number of stove vent hoods. He never asked why but suspected that it had something to do with the overhead grease trap adjacent to the ceiling light's electrical wires. He noted that clogged grease traps are highly combustible. If overloaded, the wiring to the light could arc and cause a flashover to the grease trap, which could cause the vent hood to erupt into flames, before traveling through the wiring to the electric oven and down the hall to the breaker box.

When he first moved into London Square, Gorenflo said he had his entire oven replaced after he lifted up the stove top and observed a half-inch layer of grease beneath the burner.

"I don't think they ever inspected #716," he said. "I think a lot of things were swept under the rug."

Allen Gorenflo was not alone in his observations of electrical problems at London Square. A closer look at London Square revealed a plethora of potential causes. By late 2014, as legal proceedings against Miashah dragged on, publicity about the case had reached social media and others were taking note.

12

"A fire waiting to happen"

ON January 29, 2015, a message was posted on a Moses family Facebook page by a person claiming to have information as to the real cause of the fire—and it wasn't cooking.

Three days later, Chrisandria and a small group of five huddled in a corner booth of a local café to hear a man named Famous Tankersley present a litany of electrical deficiencies in the aging complex that he claimed were ignored by London Square management and passed over by city inspectors.

"There's a young lady in jail right now who shouldn't be there," he told them.

Tankersley, owner of EWS LLC, was hired by London Square owner Paul Forkeotes as the general electrical contractor to repair building 400 and the November 2013 fire that killed Noni and Nylah Moses in building 700. "They have the wrong person in jail," he said. "I've got the electrical report. Everything's out of code." And he wasn't talking about the old 1965 electrical codes when the complex was built. He was talking about today—the electrical repairs they had just completed.

The documents Tankersley spread across the table were extensive. A plethora of engineering reports, internal emails, and technical analysis, coupled with his first-hand knowledge of serious electrical deficiencies and code violations, offered critical context for the horrendous battle the Moses family had been waging for the truth.

He said the engineering reports were to get the insurance company to pay for the electrical upgrades. "I had to prove that the electrical was so far out of compliance, so deficient, so dangerous," Tankersley said.

To hear him tell it, London Square was a dangerous tinderbox, the result of outdated wiring and breaker boxes ill-equipped to handle the enormous electrical load generated by the 24-unit buildings 50 years later. Over the course of his work, Tankersley said he found burnt wires running through live circuits inside rusted conduits with no grounding. "We were finding burnt wires left and right inside live circuits. Literally, there were melted-down raw wires inside of a circuit that is still working. Specifically, in Miashah's building they didn't have a ground. They kept losing ground and were always jerry-rigging, making it look like it had ground when it didn't. That makes your stove unsafe, too. You've got to have proper grounding. You've got to have two hot wires, a ground, and a neutral. They didn't have that. It's illegally wired," he said. "You get any kind of short in it and they go on their own. They don't need grease or food; the metal itself will melt."

Tankersley said the first electrical engineer he contacted refused to do the work, saying "it was some of the worst they had ever seen," adding he was afraid of lawsuits and trials. The engineering firm he finally hired to evaluate electrical loads prescribed no less than 800 amps per building. "In my house I have a 200-amp electric breaker box," Tankersley said. "They have the exact 200-amp breaker box running 24 apartments, plus the laundry room, plus the boilers—all of it. There's no way that can happen!"

"Each apartment has only a 60-amp Zinsco breaker," he said. "And the electric oven alone pulls 40 to 50 amps. That leaves only one additional electrical outlet before it's overloaded." Then things begin to blow. Lights flicker and circuits get fried.

It gets worse, he said. According to manufacturer hazard warnings, the original Zinsco breakers have a 25% failure rate of tripping from overloads, meaning that a failure was likely to occur in one of every four London Square apartments, many of them occupied by tenants with small children. "It should be tripping breakers," he said. "But the problem is, *those breakers won't trip. They're defective!*"

Tankersley also said it appeared that many of the 50-year-old wiring and breaker boxes were originally rated for the use of gas ovens, not electric. "It looks like somebody slipped the electric ovens in after the fact. You see gas lines stumped up. And then all of the sudden they disappear. Somebody switched them over to electric." If several tenants turned on their ovens at the same time, the lights in neighboring apartments began to dim and oven burners heated slower.

"I took out all the stoves and all the wires [from building 400]. They were all burnt. Every one of them was burnt," he said. "The reason is that you're trying to pull all this current, all the amps, when everyone's got their stoves on—and then if several tenants turned their ovens off, *whoosh!* —you have a fire! The other ovens get the brunt of the surge and things explode."

Miashah's dilemma, in Tankersley's view: She thought the stove was off and a power surge made a cool stove hot.

"It was a fire waiting to happen," he shook his head.

London Square exposed wiring at London Square (Photo: Carol Mersch)

13

Another Voice

JACK Palau was standing on top of building 400 when the fire in Miashah's unit #716 broke out.

"I was standing in the attic—most of the roof was gone—and one of the crew members said, 'There's another fire. Turn around,'" Palau remembered. "So we all turned around and there were flames coming out of the side of building 700. Smoke was pouring out of the roof." Along with Tankersley, Palau and the construction crew ran down to 700 to help tenants evacuate.

Palau had recently been hired by the owner Paul Forkeotes as the public adjuster for London Square. His job was to examine the damage from an earlier fire in building 400 and negotiate payment with the insurance company. He was now asked to negotiate the building 700 insurance claim. As an Oklahoma-licensed public adjuster, Palau took his job seriously and didn't tolerate misinformation or anything less than full disclosure. A balding, bearded man, he spoke mostly in quips.

He said that the City of Tulsa refused to allow him access to #716 for nearly a month after the fire, "which was highly unusual."

The only people allowed access were city officials and London Square personnel. "The mayor was there. The DA was there. The Chief of Police was there. The Chief of the Fire Department was there. There were people standing around with camera crews daily for weeks. There were rumors that Al Sharpton was coming, but he never showed up," he said.

After they were cleared to access building 700, Palau and Tankersley found more code violations that made the building 400 wiring seem even more suspicious. "In rooms in 700 that only had smoke damage, we were pulling out wires that had melted inside the wall and had actually started electrical fires that then put themselves out somehow," Palau said. "It was pretty obvious that there were major issues going on."

According to Palau, the same day fire investigators were on site to investigate the #716 fire, another fire broke out in a nearby unit that the London Square maintenance crew covered up. "I attempted to get into the unit to see what happened, but maintenance workers pushed me back out," he said. "I shoved my way back in." The tenant told him he had turned the burner off, and when he turned his back, "It just burst into flames." It burned up all of his cabinets and melted the pan. When maintenance workers told the tenant it was due to unattended cooking and he would be responsible for the damage, he denied the accusation and moved out.

Concerned that building 400 had been cleared for occupancy by city inspectors and that building 700 now appeared to have similar electrical problems, Palau asked the City of Tulsa's Chief Electrical Inspector John Staires to inspect buildings 400 and 700 personally. Palau told Staires the original inspector had passed things that shouldn't have been passed.

With some reluctance, Staires agreed to meet them at London Square. "He was very defensive, very gruff," Palau said. "And when he got to the 400 building his expression changed tremendously. He could not believe that his inspector allowed it to happen," said Palau. "It was actually some of the scariest work he'd ever seen on a job site, and he stated the fact: 'I need to talk to the city attorney because we're about to get sued.'"

According to Palau, after a settlement was reached on building 400 with its insurance company, they promptly dropped the London Square account. A second insurance company covered building 700 but balked at Palau's total claim amount, which included a supplemental payment for upgrades. Forkeotes hired a private attorney to force a settlement, which he eventually received.

Based on his first-hand knowledge of the insurance settlement negotiations, Palau estimates Forkeotes received over one million dollars in insurance settlements for repairs to buildings 400 and 700. "He received [the supplemental] payment to re-wire the 700 building and as far as I know he didn't rewire it, saying, 'I have other bills to pay.'"

It was a growing moral dilemma for both Palau and Tankersley.

In response to Palau's concern about the handling of the insurance money for building 700, Forkeotes assured him there would be more claims work for him in the future: "The 700 fire claim on our property last year almost put us out of business," Forkeotes said in an email. "And we have had 7 small stove fires since the last fire claim, which indicates we may be going through this process again in the future… I would be inclined to hire you again in the event we were to have another fire."

After receiving final insurance payouts, Forkeotes then terminated the services of Tankersley and Palau, leaving building 700 upgrades unfinished and their outstanding invoices unpaid.

When asked by a reporter about all the fires in London Square, Forkeotes was adamant that all stove fires were caused by tenants leaving stoves on and unattended. "Trying to blame or assume that any of the London Square fires were due to electrical issues is completely false," he said. "All fires were caused by tenants leaving their stoves unattended. None were caused by electrical wires or deficiencies. This is also the conclusion of the city inspectors."

Less than a year later, the Tulsa Fire Department responded to another fire in London Square. The fire incident report states it started in a downstairs wall below Miashah's apartment and burned across three units. The cause of the fire was listed as "Undetermined." All three units were vacant at the time.

14

A troubled past

MIASHAH'S soft voice and diminutive demeanor masked a fierce independence—a trait that had landed her in court more than once, particularly when she felt unfairly maligned. Being short, stocky, and black, she was an easy target for ridicule and harassment, and suspicion by those outside her circle. The combination led to a series of encounters with police, some brought on by her own naiveté.

Court records show she pleaded no contest to a misdemeanor assault and battery charge in 2009 at 19 after she fell into a heated argument with another girl that turned combative. Police were called, and the officer had difficulty pulling her off. Twice, after the two had been separated, Miashah lunged back after the girl.

She was twice arrested for "possession of tobacco by a minor," once in 2009 when she was of legal age but couldn't produce a driver's license because she didn't have one—she didn't drive.

Another in 2012 when a deputy as called to the Tulsa transit bus station where a security guard had pepper sprayed Miashah for an unspecified reason. The deputy conducted a pat down and found a cigarette package in her pocket. This time she gave the officer the name of her best friend as her own, and assuming from her appearance that she was underage, although she was 21, he advised her she was under arrest for possession of tobacco by a minor. The tobacco charge then became the basis for a continued frisk, during which he found "a folded piece of notebook paper in her right front watch pocket," which he said contained a small amount of marijuana. Oklahoma law defined marijuana as a controlled substance, which then resulted in an added charge against her for possession of a dangerous drug. He also found a social security card in her pocket showing her real name and added a felony charge for "impersonation to create liability."

She had no money to speak of, so court costs and fines for the arrests went unpaid for several years. By the time of the fire, her total unpaid court costs had grown to more than $5000—the equivalent of nearly a full year's rent for Keahmiee and the kids at London Square.

Added to the triple stroke of being broke, black, and gay, Miashah's case was awash in a sea of white faces: DA Tim Harris, Judge David Youll, Judge James Caputo, Assistant Sarah McAmis, and lead Prosecutor DA Kunzweiler were all white. The only person of color on the scene was Miashah's pro bono attorney, Sharon Holmes, a trim slip of a woman with a military background and a penchant for helping the less privileged. Mid-way through the case, however, Holmes was elected as Tulsa County District Court's first black female judge, which necessarily pulled her off the case.

Holmes routinely shared cases with Fred DeMier, a stocky, gruff criminal defense lawyer with an office in the same building as Holmes.

DeMier had served as a DA for 20 years in multiple Oklahoma counties and a Judge on the Oklahoma Court of Civil Appeals. With forty-seven years of experience, DeMier was well respected as a tenacious adversary and not easily intimidated. Demier was also white, which now made Miashah's courtroom cast a full white flush.

Whether or not DeMier was aware in advance that he would be assuming Miashah's case, he appeared taken aback at Holmes announcement during a meeting with Chrisandria that he would be taking over the case. He already had a caseload of pro bono clients, and while he often alternated cases with Holmes, Miashah's case did not appear to be one that he anticipated.

Even if all the officials were without a bone of prejudice, and even with DeMier, a seasoned attorney, taking on her case on a pro bono basis, Miashah was an African American with an arrest record, one who had already been portrayed in the media as a murderer. She knew it would be an uphill battle.

Considering Oklahoma is arguably one of the reddest, right-wing states in the U.S., the political climate in the community didn't bode well for assembling an unbiased jury to hear the case of a black, gay female defendant.

Chrisandria herself was so shocked when Miashah told her she was gay that she kicked her out of the house. With a handful of kids still in the house, it just wasn't something she could deal with. But the November 2013 deaths of Noni and Nylah changed all that. Having her first-born daughter accused of murdering her grandchildren forced Chrisandria to realize that Miashah's sexuality was not as important as she thought. The trauma drew them back together.

Miashah was essentially homeless when she moved into London Square with Keahmiee. Since being kicked out of her home by Chrisandria, she had been living on the streets and crashing at friends' houses where she could. With her sister and two small nieces now together under one roof, the Section 8 housing project seemed like heaven.

That is, until heaven turned to hell.

15

When foxes guard the henhouse

IT had now been nearly a year since the fire with little progress.

Frustrated and determined to understand the basis for Miashah's charges, in 2014 Keahmiee and Chrisandria sent an Open Records Request to Tulsa Fire Chief Ray Driskell, requesting all after-action reports and photos referenced by the Tulsa fire investigators at the preliminary hearing. As the mother and grandmother of the dead children, they felt they were entitled to evidence relating to the children's death, and even more important to them, the case against Miashah. The 1995 Oklahoma Open Records Act states that such citizens' requests "shall be handled promptly."

After several months with no response, Chrisandria phoned the Tulsa Fire Department records coordinator, who told her the request was "under legal review." Chrisandria continued to follow up, and she was referred to the City of Tulsa's Legal Department. She spoke to the legal department twice and received the same response each time: "Under legal review." Over a year later, the Moses family had yet to receive a response to their Open Records Request.

After receiving their complaint in January, 2015, the Fire Department's Public Information Officer Stan May suggested they forward a more specific request directly to City Attorney David O'Melia. A second Open Records Request submitted January 26, for "any and all Tulsa Fire Department after-action reports and related photographs" also went unanswered.

Perturbed by the dismissive attitude of city officials, on February 7, 2015, a concerned friend of the family contacted Tulsa City Councilor G.T. Bynum, whose district included London Square. Bynum attempted to coordinate a response from the Fire and Legal Departments but was unable to do so. Chrisandria then phoned Bynum's office administrator and asked specifically if their request was being ignored because the family was black. This prompted a phone call and personal home visit by Chrisandria's own City Councilor Connie Dodson—who also ran into a dead end.

Calls to the Tulsa Housing Authority and HUD were unproductive, and attempts to reach local NAACP and Urban League offices were to no avail; the offices had been shuttered.

Oklahoma's Open Records Act procedures were instituted in Tulsa in 1995 by executive order of Mayor Susan Savage. It therefore seemed reasonable that the mayor's office could offer direction as to the proper oversight authority. When a family member contacted Mayor Dewey Bartlett's office in late 2015, however, a spokesman stated that the office was not responsible for oversight of the Open Records Act and didn't know who was.

The pervasiveness of Oklahoma's Open Records Act violations came to light in a very public way when a 2015 nationwide study by the Center for Public Integrity awarded Oklahoma an "F" in accountability and transparency, ranking it 40th in the nation. The survey measured the difference between the laws on the books and how they're actually implemented. The probe determined that among the states with a substantive "enforcement gap," Oklahoma's gap ranked among the most significant.[56] A later report in 2019 showed little progress. The National Center for Access to Justice, a nonpartisan law and policy organization affiliated with major law firms and law schools, ranked Oklahoma dead last of all 50 states regarding access to justice.[57]

Miashah had been in jail over two years when DeMier received the DA's evidence: Miashah's interrogation, photographs, and copies of all interviews conducted at the scene. Included in the evidence was the ATF's analytical data detailing the timing, heat source, and levels of heat emanating from the source. The information was invaluable to DeMier and his partner, Charles Reese, in pinpointing a probable cause for the fire and establishing how long a grease fire would have taken to erupt on a hot burner.

Reese, a brilliant young attorney, spent days pouring over the ATF data. He had a penchant for detail and was familiar with complex fire reports. At Chrisandria's urging, DeMier and Reese agreed to meet with her to review their early findings. In the meeting, Reese cut to the bottom line—the skillet could have been left on a heated burner for ten minutes, 20 minutes, or half an hour and not have ignited the fire. The fire, he said, *was electrical.*

With the evidence from the investigators at the scene seemingly pointing to the pan on the stove as the ignition source, Tulsa Fire Department fire investigators had little reason to consider other factors that could have sparked the fire, such as corrosive conduits or wiring that can generate an arc flash with potentially deadly consequences. Arc flash temperatures are high enough to liquefy metal.

This was the very condition Gorenflo had feared with the breaker box he examined in #716—a compromised breaker that offered no defense against an arc flash initiated by faulty wiring in the stove, which, in this case, could explain the pan melted to the coils on the burner, as observed by Fire Marshall Mark Milstead in his testimony. According to Gorenflo's theory, this could account for the fire investigators' conclusion that the ignition source was the pan on the stove, when the source of the fire was actually an electrical arc—or the stove itself.

16

Legal tango

SEPTEMBER 14, 2015 was a sunny and warm morning in Tulsa as Fred DeMier made the short walk along Denver Avenue to the courthouse a block away to attend a 9:00 a.m. status hearing for Miashah's long-awaited jury trial. He felt purposeful and ready.

When the case was called, he stood before Judge Caputo and reported that he was prepared to proceed. Assistant DA McAmis, however, announced that the state wasn't ready, even though she had been on the case for nearly two years. Instead of proceeding, she offered a plea deal.

Caputo gave the attorneys two weeks to work out an agreement. The Moses family was hopeful that a reasonable compromise could mean partial exoneration for Miashah—possibly freedom. Miashah was scheduled to be transported that day from the county jail to Caputo's court room to hear the reduced charges and agree to sentencing.

At 2:00 p.m. on September 30, Miashah was ushered with a line of other female inmates into the court room chained together at the wrists in their orange jumpsuits. Miashah, the smallest of the group, was last in line, her hair closely cropped, looking like a school child. The women were clumsily seated in a row of chairs in the jury box, still shackled to one another.

One by one, a half-dozen members of the Moses family filed into the courtroom and took seats in the gallery. Kunzweiler sat slumped in a chair against a wall near the front of the courtroom intently focused on his cell phone.

At the bailiff's call of "All rise," Judge James Caputo ceremoniously entered the courtroom, followed closely behind by his shaggy white fifteen-pound dog named Bentley, who obediently took his place under the bench at the judge's feet. On occasion, when the "All rise" command was given, it was not unusual for courtroom observers to stand in anticipation, only to see the judge's door open and Bentley enter first, as if arriving in the order of significance. During court recesses, the judge could be seen striding through the foyer to the private court elevator with the fluffy canine glued to his heels. Something about the dog gave the hard-nosed judge an aura of compassion

DeMier and McAmis approached the bench amicably, both looking confident. DeMier had briefly discussed the terms of the plea agreement with Miashah, and she agreed it was the best she could do for herself and her family. Her abusive treatment in the oppressive jail environment was untenable and her family was falling apart—she wanted it to be over. The negotiated plea agreement of five years in prison and five on parole to run concurrently for two reduced counts of child neglect would at least put a light at the end of the tunnel. With credit for time served, she could be out in three years.

"Have you reached an agreement?" Caputo addressed McAmis.

"Yes, we have, Your Honor," McAmis announced, at which point Kunzweiler looked up from his cell phone.

Caputo then turned to Miashah and hesitated, "…How do you pronounce your first name?"

"Ma-ee-sha," she enunciated.

"All right, Miashah Moses," he continued. "I'm holding a waiver of trial by jury. If you will raise your right hand, please, and be sworn the best you can. Do you solemnly swear or affirm that the testimony you are about to give will be the truth, the whole truth, and nothing but the truth, so help you God?"

"Yes, sir." The wrist chains were so short that when she attempted to raise her hand, the hand of the woman on her left involuntarily raised as well. In this awkward position, she was sworn in.

He then continued with the litany of questions to verify that she was sober and sane: "Are you under the influence of any drug or alcohol?… Are you taking any medication?… Are you *supposed* to be taking medications?… Have you ever been treated for mental illness?…" He continued ad infinitum reciting the witness oath heard routinely on "Law & Order."

He then asked McAmis to state the terms of the agreement.

"We're asking for her to serve 10 years, 15 years total with ten years in and five out on each count…"

She didn't get any further.

"That's not what we agreed to," DeMier interrupted. "Your Honor, we need to withdraw that. That wasn't my understanding at all."

McAmis turned and glared at him.

They had discussed the agreement only hours earlier. A terse, hushed exchange took place as they tried to reconcile the misunderstanding. It was to no avail.

A frustrated DeMier walked to the row of chained women, knelt down and whispered intently to Miashah for several minutes. She could accept the DA's plea or move on to a jury trial. Her lengthy incarceration had done nothing to weaken her resolve—she would let a jury decide.

DeMier then left the courtroom, his jaw set, and walked straight into a crowd of waiting reporters where he gave the first hint at the defense: "It wasn't something cooking on the stove that started the fire," he said flatly. "But I really can't go into that."

As the Moses family left the courtroom, local TV crews and reporters moved in like piranhas. Up to this time, Keahmiee had avoided the cameras. Now, devastated by the plea bargain debacle, the otherwise demure and soft-spoken girl stepped in front of the cameras and delivered a strong, impassioned rebuke of the media's portrayal of her sister.

"I lost my sister. I lost my two children. I buried my two kids when I was 19. I finally came to see the reality that I have to deal with it. And it's hurt me every day," she said. "*She's my sister. She's not just a friend. She's my sister.* She's taken care of my kids for years. I had my first baby when I was only 15, and if it weren't for her, I wouldn't have graduated high school." Tears were welling up. "They've pitted me against my sister. We need time to grieve," she pleaded. "I thought I would see my sister come out free. It was an accident. It shouldn't have been dragged out this long. We haven't had a chance to grieve, and we need to grieve together."

A female reporter shoved a microphone in her face. "What does she say happened that day?"

With that, Chrisandria moved in like a mother bear. The injustice of the media and public portrayals of Miashah had gone on long enough. In April, only seven months earlier, a wealthy, 73-year-old, white Sheriff's Reserve Deputy Robert Bates had mistakenly shot and killed Eric Harris, a black man, while he was pinned to the ground by another deputy. Bates, a long-time friend and fishing buddy of Tulsa's Sheriff Stanley Glanz, was using his own unauthorized weapon. Since becoming a reserve deputy in 2008, Bates had donated thousands of dollars for vehicles, Glocks, and stun guns to the Sheriff's Department and had chaired one of Glanz's re-election campaigns. The Eric Harris case had received national attention. Whereas Bates was charged with only second-degree manslaughter for shooting an unarmed suspect point blank, Miashah was charged with second-degree murder for merely emptying the trash.

The disparity was fresh on Chrisandria's mind as she faced off with the cameras and unleashed an impassioned torrent.

"She *doesn't know* what happened that day! But what everybody should know is: This apartment complex keeps having fire after fire. Everybody in here has stepped away from their children for 6 to 8 minutes—you dump your trash, you cut your lawn, you talk to your neighbor. The real question is why is her charge second-degree murder when you have the Fire Department saying it was an accident? Everybody saying it was an accident? Then somebody accidentally shoots somebody and is only charged with second-degree manslaughter. *Now ask yourself that*!"

The reporter was taken aback. "Are you a family member?"

"I'm these girls' mother," Chrisandria shot back. "These were my grandchildren. And this is *wrong.* This is all kinds of wrong. All we get is *lies, lies, lies!…* If they want to go to trial, *bring it,*" she said, "Bring it. We're not afraid. This one they will not win."

With that, she turned, walked to a nearby elevator, and hit the down button.

17

Bunk 2, Cell 5

BY now, Miashah had been confined in Pod F-20 of the Tulsa County Jail for two years awaiting trial—a large windowless chamber lined with an upper level of bunks overlooking a common inmate gathering area. She spent most of her time watching the one television in the center common area or sitting on Bunk 2 of Cell 5, reading her Bible. Women in F-20 do not leave the pod except for meals and Sunday services or medical reasons. Snacks and outgoing phone calls come with a hefty price tag. Incoming calls to jail inmates are not accepted.

Trauma has taken its toll. When she is asked about the day of the fire, a bewildered look settles on Miashah's face. It's the same blur. Nothing's changed. When asked how she learned of the children's death, she looks vacant. She can't remember. The same is true for her arrest and questioning by detectives.

"Everything just kind of floated past me," she said of her interrogation. "I don't think they gave me the proper time to even gather my thoughts because I was in some state of shock. The only thing I remember is seeing the fire and trying to save the babies. But everything else was a blur. I don't think they really took the opportunity to really know. They just took advantage of my state of shock."

But she says she is at peace with whatever the outcome may be. "The DA doesn't care if I'm guilty or not. He only wants to convict me," she said. "I don't care what the DA wants. I don't care what the jury wants, I only care what God wants."

18

Imperfect justice

WHILE London Square's shoddy electrical work doesn't negate the fact that Miashah left two small children unattended for 8-10 minutes, childcare specialists say that for a 4-year-old and an 18-month-old, everything is unsafe without direct supervision. They could stick a fork in an outlet, or trip and fall and hit their head, or swallow household cleaner. For a curious child, everything is a potential death trap.

Way back at the preliminary hearing, the judge grappled with Assistant DA McAmis' contention that any parent who leaves a child for eight minutes can be charged with second-degree murder if the child dies.

"Would it have been neglect had a fire *not* occurred?" the judge asked.

"It could have been, Your Honor," McAmis argued.

Miashah's attorney, Holmes, zealously disputed the notion.

McAmis countered with the argument that what legally constitutes inadequate supervision in this case should ultimately be decided by a jury.

McAmis' argument may be fair and accurate, but it exists within an imperfect, inconsistent, often unfair system. Two recent similar cases in Tulsa resulted in decidedly different outcomes.

On May 2, 2014, 21-year-old Makayla Rhotenberry put her 1- and 2-year-old girls in the bathtub together and went to the kitchen to start dinner. Affidavits show the mother checked on the girls once and they were fine, but when she went back about ten minutes later, the 2-year-old was wandering in the bedroom and the youngest, Avery, was face down in the water. Makayla was charged with "failing to provide proper supervision." Bond was set at $25,000, and Makayla spent only four days in jail. She was later given four years' probation on a reduced charge of second-degree manslaughter.[58] [59] [60]

On July 1, 2014, Amber Alexander, the wife of a police officer, failed to check on her 2-year-old foster child, Mia, from 7:30 a.m. to 9:30 a.m., when she found her drowned at the bottom of the family swimming pool. The toddler had somehow gotten through an unlocked security gate and out the back door to the pool. No charges were filed against Amber. Mia was buried in a yellow dress and her favorite red shoes, and the family received an outpouring of sympathy.[61] [62]

There is no record of Amber or Makayla being patted down at the scene of their loss.

The tragedy of losing a child is no less heart-wrenching for the Moses family than for the Rhotenberry or Alexander families. The three cases have dire similarities, but with one distinguishing difference: Rhotenberry and Alexander were white.

In the Rhotenberry case, it's difficult to find a substantive difference between leaving a child in a bathtub for 10 minutes to fix dinner in the next room and leaving a child in front of a television for 8-10 minutes to take out the trash.

Amber Alexander failed to check on her two-year-old foster child for a full two hours, with back exits from the house left unsecured. Miashah Moses, meanwhile, was much more attentive to the children in the hour before the fire, feeding them and changing diapers. She then secured the door to protect against their wandering out and falling to their death like little Mia had when she fell into the pool.

How do you weigh which tragedy is more egregious? How do you compare the grief that will endure for a lifetime? Certainly not on the scales of justice. Grief knows no color. The complex labyrinth of life seldom leaves us with logical answers. We are left only with weak and uniformed hindsight.

On August 27, 2014, Tulsa ambulances responded to a 911 call from a man who left his 8-month-old baby playing in a tub. He had returned a few minutes later to find him unconscious, submerged in 6-to-8 inches of water. Thankfully, the child was revived at the hospital and recovered. Police declined to give the name of the man and no charges were filed.[63] [64]

The pivot between a lifetime of joy and one of despair can happen, quite literally, in the minutes when no one is watching.

19

Failure to communicate

TYRONE Coleman's voice rang out in the parking lot outside the Tulsa County Jail: "I would rather die standing up than live lying down." His second cousin Miashah was locked inside.

Coleman, a beefy, 39-year-old, six-foot-tall black man with shoulder-length dreadlocks was well acquainted with the seamy side of the justice system. A one-legged activist against police tactics, he was raised in north Tulsa's black community by his aunt Earleen, Chrisandria's mother, when his own mother, Amanda, was sent to Oklahoma's Mabel Bassett Prison for shooting a neighbor when Tyrone was nine. After returning to Arizona for a time and being roughed up by law Arizona enforcement, he moved back to Tulsa to be near his family. Leaning on his crutches in the parking lot of the large block building that afternoon, he wasn't sure the move had been a good one. Things weren't much better in Tulsa.

Tyrone was among those present at Miashah's preliminary hearing and heard the DA's key witness, Torrance Williams, admit that he was offered leniency on a charge of marijuana possession if he would testify against Miashah. He had come to the parking lot that fall afternoon with other family members to sign an affidavit to that effect.

A bloody accident as a teenager badly fractured his right leg when he was riding a scooter with no brakes and swerved to get out of the way of an oncoming car. A neighbor's truck was parked at the side and he crashed into the back of the truck and slid under. "But there was no excuse for amputating it," Amanda said. "The hospital let it set up to gangrene and the doctor had to remove my child's leg."

How Amanda ended up in Mabel Bassett is another story. "I did something. It was over 20 years ago," she said. "I don't regret it because it had to do with my kids. My oldest boy got in a fight with some other kids and Tyrone went off to help him. Then the older one went off and left Tyrone alone, so the other kids double-teamed him. Tyrone used to like to be everybody's friend. He was my baby. But they were always double teamin' him, threatening to kill him. And a bunch of kids came to my house and said 'Mrs. Coleman, Mrs. Coleman, they're jumping on Tyrone around there.'" Amanda's voice rose in tension as she relived the story as if it were yesterday.

"So, being me, I put my gun in my pocket and went around there. Tyrone was fighting four brothers. And their mother told them to go out and double-team my baby, Tyrone. And I told her if you sic your kids on my child, I will fuckin' shoot you. And I meant that. And I did it. I shot her! I shot her in the knee. And I admit that. And if I had to do it again, I'd do that. Don't tell your kids to come outside and jump on my baby!"

She was sentenced to eight years in the Mabel Basset Correctional Center for women. "I had never had a parking ticket or nothing like that. I had never been in trouble in Tulsa, none of that! I worked a job, every day," she said. "Oklahoma did me wrong. And when I got out of the pen, I got the hell out of Oklahoma because that's not my cup of tea. And I will never, never, ever live in Oklahoma again."

On the day of the fire, she was in Tulsa visiting her sister Earleen, Chrisandria's mother. "What they did to my niece is—excuse my language—un-fuckin' believable. Unbelievable!... I was there when the babies died November 18, and my birthday was four days later. *I will never forget that. Never, never, never.* And Miashah loved those babies. She helped raise her own sisters and her brothers. And that child would never, ever, ever do nothing to hurt those babies. Her heart is broke! And I will never, never, ever live in Oklahoma again. I've got too many memories there. They railroaded Miashah. They knew that those apartments were ratty! It was an electrical fire!"

Meanwhile, in Pod F-20, Miashah's emotional stamina was waning. Fellow inmates at the jail came and went, some more hostile than others, and as weeks stretched into months, Miashah was left to endure daily verbal abuse. According to Chrisandria, one detention officer on the floor took an open disliking to Miashah.

"She just doesn't like me," Miashah said, speaking of the white detention officer. "She just doesn't like me. I've never done anything. I do Bible study and everything. She has the prisoners that she likes, a little clique of prisoners that she talks to, and she calls me 'B.K.'"

When she asked the officer why she called her "B.K.," the officer had two words: "Baby Killer." The abbreviation became her nickname among inmates, some of whom she previously considered her friends. A jail gang mentality evolved, and she was trapped in the middle of it. Having been confined over two years in the throes of dissention, unaware of the mounting evidence of electrical wiring defects in London Square that could exonerate her, Miashah's hope for vindication was slipping away.

"What's ATF?" she asked a visitor quizzically, alluding to a comment by her attorney, Fred DeMier, about a detailed fire analysis report during his recent visit.

"Alcohol, Tobacco, and Fire," the visitor answered.

The ATF report that DeMier had referred to was a forensic fire analysis prepared by the federal agency's local office. It had been submitted as supplemental evidence to the Tulsa Fire Department. While the City Fire Department reports contained routine reporting of fire paths and heat levels in the unit, the ATF analysis gave more detailed tracking of smoke and heat intensities as the fire traveled through rooms, ceilings, and walls of the unit from its supposed source—the oven.

Miashah never saw the 40-page assembly of complex graphs. Charles Reese, DeMier's partner, believed it gave evidence that an electrical spark caused the fire instead of grease, as Assistant DA McAmis claimed. But DeMier never explained this to Miashah. The evidence for her innocence escaped her.

By this time, Miashah's jury trial had been delayed four times, and the discovery hearing, a final step in submitting evidence, had been delayed six times, and then a seventh when DeMier requested additional time to locate an electrical engineer as an expert witness. This pushed the discovery hearing dangerously close to the trial date, now only two weeks away.

Like many caught in the legal system who have no knowledge of the process, Miashah couldn't tell if they were at the end, the middle, or still at the beginning of the process. Over the past year, whenever she pressed DeMier for information and her defense options, Miashah said he told her, "You know, I'm not getting paid for this," as if he was increasingly exasperated by the prolonged pro bono case.

"He won't come to see me," she told Chrisandria during a jail visit in June, 2015. "He won't accept my phone calls. I don't know what's going on."

Chrisandria tried to intercede with DeMier on Miashah's behalf but met the same stone wall. "Anytime I call and try to talk to DeMier, he tells me, 'You're not my client. She is.' It's the same thing, every time. Neither one of us know what's going on."

"When we present our evidence to other people outside the state, they basically say, 'It's an open and shut case,' but the people here in Oklahoma obviously don't see that," she told Miashah during a jail visit. "I don't understand why they're still holding you. The Sheriff's Department is corrupt. Judge Caputo is corrupt."

She explained, "I was just trying to reassure Miashah that everything was going to be alright, and I'm running out of stuff to say, you know. Because what she was telling me is actually that Fred had another client in jail there and she was scheduled for trial the same day. How can that work? Miashah's trial will take more than a day!" Key witnesses for Miashah's defense still had yet to be notified by DeMier of the pending trial. "Not one time was I asked to testify! I volunteered," Tankersley said, frustrated at the futility of the evidence he had meticulously gathered and submitted to DeMier nearly a year earlier.

As the docket of court proceedings stretched into a tangle of 123 entries, Miashah fell into a quagmire of remorse, ultimately resigning herself to the fact that she might indeed have been responsible for killing Noni and Nylah. As is common with inmates in prolonged confinement, she began to succumb to the "code of existence"—that it is better to comply than to resist.

"If God wants me to suffer for what I've done, then I can accept that," she said in final desperation. So, when DeMier contacted her shortly before the discovery hearing and reported that McAmis had made a plea offer that would reduce her second-degree murder charge to child neglect, she took it.

The ordeal was taking a toll on her family, especially Keahmiee. Miashah phoned Keahmiee and asked if she had done the right thing. "I told her to do whatever she wants," Keahmiee said. "I just want it to be over for both of us."

In spite of mounting evidence pointing to other causes for the fire that might exonerate her, the steady march of second-degree murder proceeded down the corridors of power.

20

'Stuck in unforgiveness'

AT a candlelight vigil in the aftermath of the fatal shooting of 18-year-old Michael Brown in Ferguson, Missouri, Michelle Moulden, the pastor of Tulsa's Vernon African Methodist Episcopal (AME) Church, said, "You know why bad things happen? Because we sit and do nothing."

Metropolitan Baptist Church senior pastor Ray Owens also attended the vigil and said that everyone, regardless of their background, deserves an equal chance at a decent life. "We want to put an end to the idea that certain bodies are more valuable than other bodies," he said.

Still, the labored wheels of judicial oppression and legal intimidation ground on. Fred DeMier appeared to be growing weary of investing time and labor for no pay in a case swirling in media controversy. Evidence was still piled on his office desk waiting to be reviewed and presented at trial.

The onslaught of accusations and media pressure were unrelenting for the Moses. Financial matters and living quarters for Chrisandria's immediate family of six were always in turbulence, as was her employment. The press accosted her at every turn, always snooping for potentially disastrous news and hyping otherwise innocuous outcomes into sensational headlines. Family disagreements and resolutions came and went as relatives came to grips with the loss of their tiniest members. As the months and years passed, the dead children's birthdays were never forgotten.

When asked to describe the situation, Chrisandria crumbled. "I just don't understand the fact that they *kep*t having fires… *and kept having fires,"* she said tearfully. "And it's the same thing *every time… every time.* I mean, at the end of the day, you know, whatever happened I have to accept. And I have no problem doing that. And I know everybody's got their degrees, and they're specialists… and they know this and they know that," she wiped tears from her face. "But common sense is just common sense. I know in my gut—and whatever happens, *happens*—but I know in my spirit that something is not right with that."

Miashah was facing a possible sentence of life in prison for, in essence, locking her nieces in her apartment for safety as she took out the trash. She had spent over two years behind bars, suffering retaliation and verbal abuse with no end in sight, supposedly presumed innocent.

"It's a depressing place," she said during visiting hours in January, 2016. "One day, I'll be staring off in space, and all of the sudden I'll go back to that day. And I want to know why God put me here. I try to understand the guy—and I can't.

"I'm stuck in unforgiveness."

PART 2

MOCKERY OF JUSTICE

The DA was determined to send her to prison, but she wasn't going easily.

21

A recalcitrant DA

CHRISANDRIA wasn't giving up. She phoned the DA's office and asked for a private meeting with Kunzweiler. The meeting was scheduled for April 26, the day before Miashah's scheduled hearing.[65]

Chrisandria described the meeting.

"It was just me and Keahmiee," she said. Kunzweiler's assistant, a middle-aged woman with short brown hair, joined him at the meeting.

Keahmiee spoke first.

"I came to speak to you because you know my sister is on trial for murder for my two young daughters, and my family and I have been suffering for almost three years. I know my sister would never do anything to hurt my children, and she *didn't* hurt my children. As everybody knows, those apartments had multiple problems, yet my sister sits in jail for nearly three years for second degree murder and we just want to be done. We want to be able to heal and we can't heal without her. This is hurting me even more. I've already lost my two children, and now you guys want to take my sister. And I just came to ask you personally, as the mother of the two children, to please let her go."

According to Chrisandria, Keahmiee had barely finished her last sentence when Kunzweiler broke in. "She's not going to be released. She's going to have to do some kind of jail time. Although we know the way the fire started was questionable."

"*And I'm thinking*," Chrisandria recounted, "*If you know the way the fire started is questionable, why are you prosecuting her!? If you're acknowledging it was unsafe conditions, why in the hell aren't you doing anything about it!? There's more children that live there! There's more people who live there!*"

While admitting he was aware of other possible causes of the fire, Kunzweiler proceeded to denigrate Keahmiee.

"'Who is the father of the children?' he asked, fixing his eyes on Keahmiee.

"*Keahmiee was only able to get his first name out,*" said Chrisandria, "*when he jumped in and said,* 'Well, he's the real criminal for the simple fact that he left you—'" "See?" Chrisandria said. "*He doesn't even know what he's talking about!* Then he said, 'He left you to raise two children with no money and so that caused you to have to live in a dilapidated, unsafe'—*his exact words*—'apartment,' *implying that it was Keahmiee's fault that she lived in a dangerous apartment because, essentially, she had been impregnated by a boy who couldn't, or wouldn't, pay child support.*"

His assistant's eyes widened.

"*He did not know that!*" Chrisandria described his diatribe. "*He just made that assumption, which I felt was very disrespectful... It's about her being a woman. I don't care what color she is, it's about being a woman first! That had nothing to do with Miashah. Nothing at all to do with Miashah. But this is how disrespectful this man was.*"

"I was just trying to get him to drop Miashah's charges," Keahmiee said later. "I didn't want to be disrespectful to him, but he was disrespectful to me. He was listening, but he was talking over me."

The prospect that the DA might pursue criminal charges against the children's father hung in the air like a veiled threat. For the past twenty-seven years, Kunzweiler had served as a prosecutor in DA offices across Oklahoma. Much of his career was spent as a child enforcement attorney seeking justice for children, not only protecting minors from child neglect and abuse, but prosecuting deadbeat fathers who didn't pay child support.

But in Chrisandria's opinion, Miashah's case was not about child support, it was not about child neglect, it was about performing a routine household task in the proper care of children—feeding them lunch and taking out the trash.

Blaming a child's mother for the inactions of the father, and, more specifically, for the downstream effect on the child's living conditions, while at the same time prosecuting charges stemming from that same situation, was to Chrisandria the worst form of hypocrisy.

"You could feel the evil," Chrisandria said, describing that atmosphere. "He was so cold and so evil. And he said, 'You know I'm a *Catholic* and I have three daughters, and I'm a grandfather too.'"

Chrisandria thought to herself, "*Well, you're a Catholic-ass devil. The Bible says 'Thou shalt not judge.' That's what the Bible says. And you don't have the right to judge anyone. You don't know anything about me. You don't know anything about Keahmiee. You don't know anything about Keahmiee's baby daddy or Miashah. I'm sure it does not affect you, because you have not cried one day for my grandchildren. You have not cried one day about my daughters. This is no skin off your back. We're just a file to you. That's all we are. You just want to prosecute.*"

What actually came out of her mouth was different.

"Well, with that being said, and if you're a man of God, you should want to help heal her as much as you can. You have the power to do that. You have the power to give her a little relief, you know, to give my family a little relief."

She remembered, "*I was stunned by the fact that he had charged Miashah with second-degree murder—and then Robert Bates moonlighting as a reserve officer shoots and kills an unarmed man point blank and is only charged with second-degree manslaughter! That makes no sense to me!*"

The Bates case received national news coverage a year earlier in April, 2015, when a police body camera showed an undercover gun buy sting gone wrong. The suspect, Eric Harris, a 44-year-old black man, fled on foot and was tackled to the ground by deputies. Bates, a 73-year-old white reserve deputy, claimed he mistook his personal handgun for his Taser and shot Harris point blank in the back while he was pinned to the ground by another deputy. Harris died from the gunshot.

Harris was seen gasping on the video, "I can't breathe."

"Fuck your breath," the officer astride him muttered, not realizing Harris had been fatally wounded by Bates, whose bullet had blown a hole through Harris's armpit, ricocheted off his ribs, and pierced a hole through his lung the size of a golf ball. The 24-year-old Deputy Michael Huckeby is shown in a video kneeling on Harris' head as the dying Harris is told, "You shouldn't have ran," and "Shut the fuck up."[66]

The case was seen by many as bold-faced racism. Bates was charged with second-degree manslaughter, but the general consensus of those in the black community was that Bates would likely be exonerated.

"Well, we're not going to talk about other cases," Kunzweiler responded to her flatly.

Sitting in Kunzweiler's meeting room, confronting him face to face about the discrepancy, Chrisandria bore down: "Well, I'm talking about it," she said. "Because when I look at this as a grandmother that lost two grandbabies and a daughter that's sitting in jail for second-degree murder—being torn down by the media, my family's name being dragged through the mud—for him to be charged with second-degree manslaughter for shooting a gun—he shot a gun!—and you're alleging that my daughter left a pot on the stove for—*let's be clear*—6 minutes and 27 seconds, for walking out the door that you and I do every day? Every day you and I do this! At the end of the day, the fact is that even the Fire Department called it an accident. And for her to be charged with murder when even the Fire Department called it an accident, makes no sense to me. *There's some underlying mess going on here.*"

She described Kunzweiler as essentially blaming everybody else for the fire and the children's death except London Square. "He was like, 'I'm the big bad DA and I can do whatever I want,'" she said. "He wouldn't look at me. Every time I confronted him, he would look at Keahmiee, who was crying, and berate her mercilessly. You could tell he loved to see fear. He kept looking at Keahmiee."

"*And then he tells me in the next breath:* 'If your daughter goes to trial, I can almost *guarantee*'— and he went back and repeated—'*I can guarantee* she's going to get at least 60 years.'"

"Well, how can you tell me that if a jury is going to be picked?" Chrisandria asked. "That means you must know something I don't know."

"I don't know who the jury is going to be," Kunzweiler said.

"Well, you must know something. If you can guarantee a conviction, *then you know something*!" Despite their pleas for leniency in light of the extenuating circumstances, "Ku-Klux-Klanzweiler," as Chrisandria referred to him, remained in trenchant opposition.

"Keahmiee was crying so much she couldn't even talk," Chrisandria said. "We aren't begging anymore." They departed Kunzweiler's meeting room, leaving his assistant looking astonished.

Miashah's hearing for her guilty plea was the next morning.

22

The plea trap

AT 9:00 a.m., Miashah was once again led into Judge James was Caputo's courtroom chained to a handful of other inmates, some dressed in orange, the more troublesome ones in black and white stripes.

Kevin Leroy Smith was one of those in stripes. A fifty-one-year-old raspy, bearded man, Smith was accused of raping a twelve-year-old girl. He was transported to Caputo's courtroom from the Marion Federal Prison in Illinois, where he was already serving a 17-year sentence for possession and distribution of child porn.

Smith's rape case was heard first. His public defender, Ryan McDonald, a tall, slim, earnest man in a dark suit and stylish red tie, stood next to him in the jury box. McDonald advised Judge Caputo of Smith's decision to accept a "blind plea," in which the accused would avoid a jury trial and throw himself at the mercy of the court to decide his fate.

Assistant DA Sarah McAmis was there to prosecute both Miashah's case and the Smith case. She strode back and forth across the courtroom, gesturing passionately and arguing vigorously as she described in graphic detail the events of that day in January, 2013, when Smith abducted the shy grade-schooler as she walked home from school in Glenpool, Oklahoma, a small community south of Tulsa, and what he did to her, pushing her into his truck and driving her to a construction site where he unzipped his pants, fondled her, and took pictures of her. When confronted by a woman, he put the girl back in the truck and drove her to a location behind a residence, where he forced her to perform oral sex and raped her. He then drove her back to her neighborhood, gave her forty dollars, and shoved her out of the truck.[67]

The rape case against Smith had gone unsolved for two years until the DNA sample taken for his earlier child porn case linked him to the rape.[68]

The young victim, now 14, sat with her family on a bench at the back of the gallery weeping, her long blonde hair draped across her shoulders. McAmis read a short letter written by the girl, a description of the ongoing effect the trauma has on her day-to-day school life, frightened, embarrassed, and always looking over her shoulder: "I have been bullied because of this. I have been called names like 'whore' and 'prostitute.' I have no friends because of it."[69]

Her father was then allowed to speak. He rose and choked back emotion as he recounted to Caputo the emotional devastation inflicted on the family by the rape, saying he could no longer let his children walk home from school. "I think about the incident every day," he said, describing a period he described as "pure hell."

After testimony from the two arresting officers and numerous objections by Smith's attorney, Caputo sentenced Smith to 120 years in prison. Taken aback by the harsh sentence, Smith reacted violently and was led struggling from the courtroom by two deputies.[70]

After the rape conviction, charges against the inmate seated next to Miashah were presented: two counts of the armed robbery of two women at knifepoint. A docile young white girl with long dark hair, she pleaded guilty and waived her right to trial, leaving her sentence at Caputo's disposal. Caputo advised her of the option of serving time in prison or attending a women's recovery program, after which she would be released on probation. She quickly agreed to the recovery option.

Negative currents seeping into the atmosphere from the graphic rape case and armed robbery of two women were palpable in the courtroom. It was against this backdrop that Miashah's case was about to be heard. Even before the opening remarks, the extensive publicity of Miashah's case—of "two little girls left locked in an apartment to burn to death"—had tainted Miashah with guilt.

McAmis rose and approached the bench.

"This is déjà vu," Caputo said, smiling down at her.

Caputo was an ally of DA Steve Kunzweiler's, and for whatever reason seemed to pay special deference to his Assistant DA Sarah McAmis' courtroom appearances.

DeMier promptly stepped to the bench next to her and addressed the judge: "At this time, Ms. Moses would enter a plea of guilty to both counts."

"Thank you," Caputo said, turning to Miashah seated on the prisoner bench.

"Originally, ma'am, you were charged with Murder in the Second Degree in Commission of a Felony in both Counts 1 and 2," Caputo said. "I'm informed by the State of Oklahoma and your attorney that those charges are being amended to Child Neglect as described in 21 O.S.843.5(C)."

"Is that correct, Ms. McAmis?" he asked, turning to McAmis.

"Yes."

"Do you understand that if I accept your pleas today, you are giving up the trial rights…?" Caputo asked Miashah.

"Yes, sir," she said.

She understood her general plea to be "failure to protect from harm." She was too worn down and weary to understand the connotation of Statute 21 O.S.843.5(C): "causing, procuring or permitting of a *willful or malicious act* of *child neglect*." She would never have willfully or maliciously caused harm to Noni and Nylah. The statute she was prosecuted under had never been explained to her. She had relied solely on DeMier to represent her best interests.

With this, DeMier walked briskly to the jury box, took a seat next to Miashah on the prisoner bench, and began hurriedly flipping through the lengthy eight-page plea agreement, scanning the 130-plus lines of fine print and pointing to sixty scribbled entries he had already completed on her behalf, including thirty-nine items circled "yes" or "no." Miashah stared intently. She had never laid eyes on the form before and was now being asked to agree to something she had never reviewed. With DeMier at her side waiting—and with the proceedings on hold as she weighed her decision—she signed the form. The entire process took just over five minutes. Miashah had no idea what she had just pled to.

After a brief recess, Caputo read her signed guilty plea out loud.

"'I was babysitting my two nieces on 11/18/13 in Tulsa County, Oklahoma, and left a skillet cooking on the stove and left for a few minutes to take out the trash. A kitchen fire started and my nieces died. I was neglectful and should not have left them. I am responsible for my neglect.'"

Caputo turned to McAmis. "The amendment carries a range of punishment of... is it still one to life?"

"Zero to life," McAmis answered.

"Zero to life," Caputo repeated.

"...or in the county [jail] one year," DeMier interjected.

"Zero to life or one year in the Tulsa County Jail," Caputo corrected. "And a fine of up to $5,000 on each of those two counts. Do you understand the counts as amended, the ranges of punishment, including the fines?"

"Yes, sir," Miashah responded.

"I show you've got an agreement as to both counts, five to be probated?" Caputo said, looking again at McAmis.

"Correct."

"...Credit for time served with a $500 fine and a $250 Victims Compensation Fund Assessment... 85 percent still?" directed once again to McAmis, as if McAmis was calling the shots.

"Yes," she answered.

"...which means you'll have to complete 85 percent of that first 10 years before you become eligible for any good-time credit or early release probation or parole... Is that your understanding of the agreement?"

"Yes, sir," Miashah answered.

He then concluded by reading the closing paragraph covering her right to withdraw her guilty plea:

"And those signatures indicate that you understand that you have 10 days from today to file an application to withdraw your plea. If you do so, I'll grant you a hearing within 30 days on that issue, and if you are not pleased with the result of that hearing, you'll then have *ten days* to appeal my decision to the Court of Criminal Appeals. Do you understand those appeal rights?"

"Yes, sir."

With that, the trap was set. While Caputo's statement may have seemed straightforward enough, legal minds in the courtroom were keenly aware that Judge Caputo could—and frequently did—deny a defendant's request to withdraw a guilty plea based on reasoning of his own.

As the hearing closed, Chrisandria rose and walked out of the courtroom, took a seat on the bench outside the door, and wept uncontrollably. After regaining her composure, she stood, wiped her eyes, and walked into the foyer to face the cameras.

23

Confused culpability

LESS than 20 feet across from Caputo's courtroom, the case of Reserve Deputy Robert Bates in the death of Eric Harris had just concluded, resulting in defendants, prosecutors, and observers from both courts mingling together in the foyer outside the courtroom. Moments earlier, Eric's brother, Andre Harris, had finished testifying in courtroom 501 directly across the hall from Miashah's hearing in 506.

When Chrisandria entered the foyer, she walked into a crowd of court spectators and news crews eager to cover results for both high-visibility cases. The media frenzy resulted in Chrisandria and Andre conducting on-camera interviews adjacent to each other, generating momentary confusion as television news crews debated over where to point their cameras.

Miashah's guilty plea hearing concluded at roughly the same time a guilty verdict was handed down in the Bates case. As both courts adjourned, Miashah was led past news crews in handcuffs, smiling at her family, visibly relieved to be rid of the legal suffering. Bates' exit was noticeably different. When Bates' guilty verdict was pronounced a short time later, he was quickly shuttled away from the crowd and disappeared down the back stairway, avoiding the press.

Chrisandria left the courthouse and was about to cross the street when she said a bailiff from the Bates trial came running out and stopped her. "Your lawyer did a shitty job," he said. "You need to hire yourself another attorney and ask them to go back in and ask for a one-year review. Your attorney should have done that." A one-year review is a formal request for the sentencing judge to review her sentence and modify it—usually to a lesser sentence or probation. But Chrisandria had done all she could. It was obvious a one-year review by Caputo would be fruitless. And Miashah was in no mood to ever lay eyes on the judge again.

Although relieved to be rid of the legal suffering, Miashah's relief proved short-lived. She had no sooner returned to her jail cell than doubts began to take hold. What she thought would be a great sense of relief was replaced with a sinking feeling. She phoned Chrisandria and said, "I feel double-minded about it." She wondered if she had done the right thing. Chrisandria told her she wasn't sure either.

It didn't go unnoticed by legal minds in the courtroom that Miashah was never specifically told by Caputo, nor informed by DeMier, that she was swearing to have "knowingly and voluntarily entered" into the guilty plea—that she was fully informed of the facts. But she couldn't have known what she didn't know.

During this time, DeMier was assisting a number of paying clients and other pro-bono defendants and had yet to fully investigate Tankersley's claims of dangerous conditions at London Square and in Miashah's apartment. Tankersley said he visited DeMier's office and personally handed him the electrical engineering analysis of overloaded breaker panels and electrical circuits. It was a deadly link to a lurking time bomb. But DeMier had never shown Tankersley's findings to Miashah. They sat in a pile of evidence on his desk for months.

Locked in Pod F-20 inside the impenetrable walls of a windowless world, there was no way Miashah could have known.

In a 2015 Tulsa City Council meeting, Jack Henderson, a long-time representative from the city's predominantly black area, cautioned city officials: "Once we admit it, we can deal with it. If we keep trying to say there's no racial divide in the city, there's always going to be racial divide." This statement was directed to an overly optimistic group of city and county officials, including DA Kunzweiler, who were extolling Tulsa's peaceful record on race relations.

During the meeting, Kunzweiler alluded to Tulsa's progress in race relations from the 1921 Race Massacre to the 2012 Good Friday random shooting in Tulsa of five black people at four north Tulsa locations by Alvin Watts and Jacob England, both white, and the more recent shooting of Eric Harris by reserve deputy Robert Bates in 2015. "This community can teach the rest of the country how to deal with this problem. We really can," he said, acclaiming his first-term accomplishments in restoring racial equality as Tulsa's new DA.

Kunzweiler was campaigning for reelection in 2018.

His statement was overshadowed two months later, when on September 17, 2015, Terence Crutcher, a 40-year-old unarmed black man, was gunned down by a white Tulsa police officer, Betty Shelby. Crutcher was seen falling to the ground with his hands raised. Marq Lewis, a black spokesman for local activist group We The People Oklahoma, called on Kunzweiler to recuse himself from the investigation due to his tight relationship with local law enforcement, saying, "We don't trust him."

"Tough laws and more police are not enough," Kunzweiler boasted in his campaigning. "A skilled and experienced prosecutor *must finish the job in court* to take dangerous criminals off our streets and keep neighborhoods safe." He was widely noted as one of the strongest opponents of criminal justice reform, fearing it would unleash these dangerous criminals back on the streets.

His Republican rival was Ben Fu, a former assistant district attorney now working in private practice. Fu said on multiple occasions that Kunzweiler's leadership fostered a culture of upping the charges filed against defendants, which sets people up for failure when they can't afford to pay high court costs and struggle to gain employment. While Fu's statements may have been accurate, they didn't work. Kunzweiler won.

In a TV broadcast after his re-election, Kunzweiler described his priorities: "The role of a prosecutor is to teach people the morals they either never learned or forgot. You have to look at every case in every set of situations individually. You can't say this case is like every other case. I want to make sure if there are people committing crimes, if they're violent crimes we get them off the street."

Whether feeding two youngsters' lunch and leaving to throw a diaper in the trash is a "violent crime" as alluded to by Kunzweiler was debatable

24

Let's get this straight

THE chairs at the table in the glass-walled conference room were occupied by a lawyer at each end. The attorneys agreed to meet with Chrisandria and Courtney to discuss the Moses civil suit against London Square owners for damages in the wrongful deaths of Noni and Nylah—a move Chrisandria hoped would serve to condemn the entire apartment complex and see it torn to the ground.

The attorney at the end of the conference table blurted out his quick, concise analysis of Miashah's case: "The judge in the case is corrupt, the fire chief is worthless, and the district attorney is flat-out crazy."

It was late afternoon on May 12, 2016, and he had heard just enough in the meeting with Chrisandria and Courtney to draw a cryptic analysis of the situation—the DA's stance in the case, the judge's leanings, and the Moses family's troubled quest to hold London Square accountable as prime malefactors in the death of the Noni and Nylah. "Once that corruptness gets in your system, it never gets out until you're carried out," he said.

Attorney Dan Smolen of Smolen & Roytman was currently pursuing a civil suit by the Harris family against Reserve Deputy Robert Bates, the Tulsa Sheriff's Department, and Sheriff Stanley Glanz personally for the wrongful shooting death of Eric Harris. Seated at the table with Chrisandria and Courtney was Andre Harris, a virtual duplicate of his murdered brother Eric Harris. Before the final investigation and guilty verdict in the Bates case, the Sheriff's Office had investigated Eric's shooting and declared Bates blameless. Given Tulsa's tortured history of race relations stemming as far back as the 1921 Tulsa Race Massacre, the activist group We the People Oklahoma, led by vocal black citizen Marq Lewis, gathered 8,000 signatures on a petition demanding a grand jury investigation of the Sheriff's Office. Dan Smolen, a principal in Smolen, Smolen & Roytman, agreed to prosecute the case.

The Bates case was assigned to Judge James Caputo.

Caputo originally denied any foregone prejudice in the case, but he failed to disclose a blatant conflict of interest before the trial. When Bates pleaded not guilty in July, 2015, Caputo gave him permission to leave the State of Oklahoma to vacation in the Bahamas. As a matter of judicial practice, defendants in manslaughter cases are specifically precluded from leaving the state without approval of the court, which Caputo had willingly granted.

The conflict didn't stay hidden for long. A court document filed in October, 2015, disclosed that Caputo had known Tulsa County Sheriff Stanley Glanz for more than 24 years and was himself once a reserve deputy who had served alongside as Robert Bates. And another inconvenient fact: Caputo's daughter was a civilian employee of the Sheriff's Office. After a watch group of investigative reporters at *The Frontier*, a Tulsa online news source, revealed the conflicts, Caputo reluctantly recused himself and Bates vacation was cancelled.

The case was reassigned to Judge Sharon Holmes, who also recused herself due to campaign contributions she received from Smolen, Smolen & Roytman. The case was reassigned to a third district judge, William Musseman, who had no conflict of interest. A grand jury was impaneled in late 2015, and Glanz was indicted on two misdemeanors. In order to avoid termination after his 27 years as a police officer, he resigned immediately. Dan Smolen eventually settled a federal civil rights lawsuit with Harris's estate for five million dollars.

Andre Harris had connected with Courtney on Facebook and was sympathetic to Miashah's plight. Andre recommended the Smolen law firm as the best-qualified organization to navigate the legal machinations inherent in a court system biased against aggrieved minority defendants such as Miashah.

Because Smolen, Smolen & Roytman had recently taken on several other civil cases, however, they suggested that the Moses family contact Sacra Law in Tulsa to handle the proposed suit against London Square. That week, Courtney and Chrisandria visited Damon Sacra of Sacra Law, who shared cases jointly with the Oxford-Leher law firm.

In November, 2015, Keahmiee Moses and the children's father, Tyler Rentie, filed a civil suit against London Square Apartments and the manufacturers of Zinsco breakers for the wrongful deaths of Noni and Nylah. The suit named six manufactures of electrical components as defendants along with London Square owners: London Square LLC and National Holdings LLC, headquartered in Abu

Dhabi, United Arab Emirates. Among the list of those charged with the manufacture of parts in the Zinsco breakers were GTE, Sylvania, Westinghouse, Challenger Electrical, Eaton Electrical, and Cutler Hammer. Paul Forkeotes, also a part owner and the complex manager with ultimate culpability, was charged separately as an individual.

The filing against London Square was lengthy, but boiled down to a brief set of facts as stated in case CJ-2015-4105 for the wrongful death of Noni and Nylah:

COMMON FACTS

> Unbeknownst to the Plaintiff or Miashah Moses, the London Square Apartments contained wiring and electrical components manufactured by Zinsco Defendants that were notoriously defective and extremely dangerous. However, the Landlord Defendants were well aware of the dangerous conditions of the wiring in the Apartment, but consciously chose not to upgrade or properly maintain the wiring, and further chose not to warn the Plaintiffs of the hidden danger.

NEGLIGENCE

> The Landlord Defendants, as owners of London Square Apartments, owed a duty to their tenants to keep the premises in reasonably safe condition for occupation, and to otherwise warn their tenants of unseen and hidden danger existing in the

> premises… and as a direct and proximate result of their failure, Noni Moses and Nylah Moses lost their lives in the ensuing fire.

The defendants cited in the civil suit were behemoth companies with deep pockets who operated on a national scale. The Tulsa law firms would need tenacity.

25

Resurrection of hope

MIASHAH was despondent, her head down, eyes focused on the concrete floor of her cell, still feeling the weight of culpability in the death of the toddlers when a voice from the front desk said someone had logged in to see her. The visitor brought two new documents not previously submitted as evidence that spoke in blunt terms to the cause of the fire.

The visitor plastered the documents one at a time against the Plexiglas of the visitor stall. One was an email from Famous Tankersley, openly frustrated that Miashah entered a guilty plea when he had gone out on a limb to turn over personal emails from London Square's owner and critical engineering reports to her attorney over a year earlier—documents that he felt would exonerate her.

"Dumbest thing she could have done was to accept the plea!" wrote Tankersley. "I can't fix stupid. No helping her now. Kind of hard to get retrial or mistrial on a plea deal! That's why prosecutors love plea deals!… That apartment [#716] was the very one management pointed out to me personally as the one where he had to Jerry

Rig [sic] the circuits to show they had ground… No offense, but London Square was and still is a death trap!!!!"

Tankersley's email was accompanied by an email from insurance adjuster Jack Palau. He wrote, "Let's not forget the fact that another unit in the same building burned within a month of that fire… A tenant had burned up his kitchen by simply turning his stove off and as the tenant said, 'it just burst into flames.'"

This was another case of faulty underpowered wiring. The oven was the last in line and took the brunt of the surge. Cindy Struder, an Arkansas resort owner who learned of the case, was aware of the dangerous conditions. "I was one of the first to manage London Square in the 1980s. The wiring was already an issue at that time and the load on the system was much less in the 1980s than today, but it seems the problems that were merely a nuisance then, have turned deadly."[71]

All of this was news to Miashah. Knowing she may not have been the cause of the fatal fire restored her dwindling sense of self-worth and hope of freedom outside the jail walls. It wasn't neglect that killed her nieces—it was the firetrap she lived in.

"I could be exonerated!" she told the visitor, almost jubilantly. "Let me show you something." She jumped from her chair and left the visitor cubicle, returning with two pieces of paper, pressing the first against the Plexiglas. It was a prepared statement given to her by Fred DeMier showing the litany of punishments she would face if she refused the DA's guilty plea—a brutal interrogation in front of a jury, life behind bars, and a barrage of other grim outcomes. This kind of intimidation through the presentation of doomsday scenarios is a common tactic used to convince defendants to accept guilty pleas.

The second was a May, 2016, news article from the *Tulsa World* newspaper only two days earlier. The large-print headline read, "Woman gets suspended sentence in DUI-related ATV crash that killed two-year-old daughter." The article described an auto accident in a nearby county caused by Angela Russell, who was driving drunk and crashed, killing her two-year-old daughter, who was strapped to her chest.[72] Miashah felt that this case was far more egregious than her own. Instead of landing behind bars, Russell received a 25-year suspended sentence and walked free.

"Did you see this?" Miashah asked. "She was charged with second-degree murder for child neglect—the same as me!"

"Yes, but the judge will say that's in a different county," the visitor said.

"But its statutory law!" Miashah shot back. "It's Oklahoma law!"

The unspoken difference was that Angela Russell was white.

By this time, Miashah was in the eighth day of the ten-day window to file a plea withdrawal. She had precious little time to reverse course. To complicate matters, it was late Friday, and the courts were closed for the weekend. Sunday would be the tenth day. However, Oklahoma criminal procedures stipulate that if the tenth day falls on a weekend, the following Monday counts as the tenth day. She had one extra day. The clock was ticking.

Inmates in the Tulsa County Jail are not permitted random phone calls to their attorneys, and she had no easy way to contact DeMier. What she did have was enough money in her phone account for a pre-authorized call to her family, which she made. Courtney answered the phone.

Panic set in with the family.

On Sunday morning, after several tries, Courtney finally reached DeMier on his cell phone and told him Miashah wanted to withdraw her guilty plea. That afternoon, DeMier visited Miashah in jail and submitted a petition for plea withdrawal to be filed when the courts opened on Monday, May 9.

Her petition cited "inadequate counsel" by DeMier for failing to make her aware of the pervasive electrical conditions in London Square—a situation brought directly to her attention by emails from Tankersley and Palau. The evidence was germane to the very crux of her plea agreement. In spite of their repeated calls to DeMier and reports by a licensed electrician showing severe amperage overloads that could trigger the faulty breaker box in #716, neither were ever contacted by DeMier. Had Miashah been aware of the evidence concerning the dangerous electrical conditions that could potentially exonerate her at trial, she would never have consented to the guilty plea.

According to Oklahoma law, worthy scenarios for withdrawing a guilty plea arise when "new evidence of innocence surfaces" or "the defendant appears to have a viable chance at trial." The meaning of the term "child neglect" as set forth in the Oklahoma Criminal Code is "the willful and malicious neglect" of a minor child.[73] The DA had selected a narrow, ambiguous sentence of the child neglect statute to flog Miashah into submission, a legal equivalent of the European torture wheel used in the 1800s to coerce prisoners into submission by strapping them to a giant wooden wheel and progressively stretching them until they either gave in or were ripped apart.

Compared to the thousands of other women unfairly impounded, Miashah was one of the fortunate ones. Others without means, outside contacts, or without dogged family members like

Chrisandria and to reach out beyond the jail walls, were left on the judicial wooden wheel.

Having barely filed a last-minute plea withdrawal, Miashah was caught in a legal conundrum. With DeMier's removal from the case, she was now left without legal representation to argue her plea withdrawal. To make matters worse, while Oklahoma criminal statutes allow 30 days for a judge to schedule a hearing for a plea withdrawal, Judge Caputo had set it for the following Tuesday, May 17, 2016, at 9:00 am, a move viewed by the Moses family as "willful and malicious" intent by Caputo himself to impede Miashah's right to due process.

After contacting several Tulsa lawyers who declined to take the case, Dan Smolen, Eric Harris's attorney in the Robert Bates civil suit, referred Chrisandria and Courtney to an attorney who sometimes represented clients in similar circumstances. Tom Mortensen was a smooth, outspoken, tenacious attorney, known to have sharp elbows in the courtroom.

Mortensen was initially skeptical and typically demanded a fee from his clients, but said he would consider taking the socially-charged case as a "righteous cause" on two conditions: one, that Miashah was committed to her innocence; and two, that she was willing to see the case all the way to a jury trial without settling for a compromise with the DA.

Miashah agreed.

Unfortunately, Mortensen was home with a severe case of bronchitis in the week leading up to the hearing. He arrived back in his office at 8:00 a.m. on the morning of May 17, one hour before the scheduled 9:00 a.m. hearing. The young, bearded attorney was sitting behind his cluttered desk dressed in shorts and a printed T-shirt, still recovering from the debilitating illness that had knocked his entire legal docket off his calendar. He was unaware of the plea withdrawal hearing that morning and had yet to even formally accept the case when Chrisandria and Courtney appeared in his doorway.

He also knew that a request for a plea withdrawal under Oklahoma law could be troublesome, especially those involving Judge Caputo and Assistant DA Sarah McAmis, with whom he had had several contentious encounters. There was no love lost between Mortensen and McAmis.

McAmis had been a prosecuting attorney with the Tulsa District Attorney's Office for 23 years specializing in child abuse cases. She was employed by the DA's office to do one thing: prosecute defendants, primarily those accused of child abuse, to the full extent of the law. Her brass-knuckles, take-no-prisoners philosophy was well known among spectators and participants in Tulsa criminal courts. She was known for flailing her arms about and accusing defendants of crimes and offenses so reprehensible that the mere mental images she conjured up were often too graphic for juries or judges to overlook.

An attractive, full-figured 43-year-old divorced woman, she could reel out legal arguments like a sausage machine.

What happened next was akin to a scene from *Batman.*

26

Legal standoff

WITH only half an hour to change clothes and with no real background on the case, Mortensen was standing in Caputo's courtroom at 9:00 a.m. to argue for Miashah's plea withdrawal. The change in appearance was stark. The disheveled individual they had seen little over an hour earlier, looking scrambled in a wrinkled T-shirt and shorts, looked nothing like the well-suited man in a pressed shirt and tie who had just risen to approach the bench.

"Who is that?" Chrisandria asked a family friend seated next to her in the gallery. They had visited Mortensen together only an hour earlier.

"That's Miashah's new attorney, Tom Mortensen."

It took her a minute to reconcile the disparity. Judge Caputo, however, knew exactly who he was.

"The State of Oklahoma is present and represented by Ms. Sarah McAmis," Caputo began, "and Ms. Moses is present and represented by Mr. Thomas Mortensen."

Mortensen briefly presented key factors of Miashah' plea withdrawal based on new evidence not previously known.

Caputo's mindset was obvious from the outset. Despite the fact that Mortensen had little advance notice to gather evidence, file an appearance, or otherwise prepare for a case he was totally unfamiliar with, Caputo denied his request for a delay to familiarize himself with the issues. Instead, Caputo ordered him back in court after the lunch recess at 12:30 p.m., apparently viewing a lunch break adequate time for a new lawyer to prepare grounds for a plea withdrawal. Miashah's family saw this as clear evidence that Caputo wanted to sabotage Miashah's effort to salvage justice. Although legally allowed 30 days to mount a plea withdrawal defense, of the 20 days remaining, Caputo was allowing Mortensen only one.

Having thrown a spear in the ground seemingly to deter Mortensen's arguments, Caputo then stood and exited the chamber door behind him. His fluffy dog Bentley followed close behind.

Mortensen raced back to his downtown office and frantically gathered evidence from DeMier's files showing London Square electrical defects and the explosive emails Miashah received from Tankersley and Palau after her guilty plea, documents that specifically pointed to faulty wiring in her unit as being not only dangerous but potentially deadly. An hour later, he was back in Caputo's courtroom prepared to proceed.

At 12:30 p.m. Caputo called the Court to order: "Let's go on the record in CF-2013-5838, State of Oklahoma versus Miashah Chantell Moses. Is the defense ready to proceed?"

Chrisandria sat in the center of the front gallery bench, her legs crossed and her foot jiggling so nervously it shook the entire bench. So much so that the heads of those seated on either side could be seen bouncing in rhythm.

Mortensen rose.

"Judge, I'm entering an appearance this morning. I have not yet filed a written entry of appearance. Earlier, I asked for additional time to present and to be able to present witnesses and evidence based on what I believe to be newly discovered evidence in this case that may have materially affected the plea in this case. The Court declined that request... I would again, at this time, orally re-urge a motion granting me to be able to present the witnesses associated with the documents I intend to introduce."

Caputo deflected the proposition. "Okay. And based on the in-chambers conference and the disclosure of what that material may be, if it was to be found, doesn't appear to have any determining factor on the defendant's decision to take the plea or not to take the plea, so I'm ready to proceed. You are re-urging it now, *and I'm denying it at this time.*"

Mortensen persisted. "Yes, sir, and I'm orally re-urging my request to amend the motion to withdraw plea to include a claim of newly discovered evidence."

Caputo wasn't having it. "Well, since I've already denied the introduction of any newly discovered evidence, this is about a motion to withdraw a plea, not about evidence, *so I'll deny that as well.*"

"I don't mean to interrupt you," Mortensen interjected. "I have shown the defendant Ms. Moses those documents and she has confirmed with me that she has not seen those documents or read its allegations or knows the contents therein."

McAmis rose and moved in like a barracuda. "The State would assert, first and foremost, that this has no relevance in a motion to withdraw a plea... It absolutely does not matter... Defendant's previous defense counsel, Mr. DeMier, for the past three years has alleged that this was an accidental fire, and that the defendant was not responsible for the fire… What the State has alleged from the very beginning is that the children perished, and the defendant's negligence based on the fact that she left two children alone and unsupervised, she dead-bolted the door, and she went to another area of the apartment complex, such that while they were alone and unsupervised and had absolutely no way to leave or get out of the apartment, the apartment caught fire, and they perished in that fire."

Mortensen anticipated McAmis' tactic. "Respectfully disagreeing, it's important for the *defendant if she believed herself to be the cause of this fire*, if she believed herself to be the original reason of why these children perished to begin with, then that is important to her at the time of her earlier plea. It's important to her on her basis, her understanding of why she pled guilty to begin with. We're not here to try the case. We're here to—if you'll indulge me—to look into the mind of the defendant and inspect the basis of what reason she had at the time of her plea, what led to it. If she learns after she had entered her plea that in fact, she was not the cause of the fire, then the only remaining charge left to ask a jury about, is whether or not they believe the time away from these children rises to the level of the lack of supervision, or rises to the level of felony negligence?

"From my understanding – which I would agree from coming in at the very last minute in this case—from what I understand, she wasn't gone from the apartment complex… from the apartment itself for five or six minutes or seven minutes… if she left believing that she had left the children in a safe environment five, six, seven minutes in an environment which they would not be subject to harm, if she truly felt that and believed that, then I don't believe that she has the *mens rea*, or the culpability that child neglect typically presents.

"The only thing she's asking for is that which is afforded every single prisoner in a judicial system—and that is to try this case to a jury of her peers. That's the only thing she's asking... She has now, based on this new evidence and these new documents presented to her, has come to the realization that she was not at fault for the fire and has decided to proceed further... And Your Honor is very well aware of the fact that all we're here to determine is whether or not she *knowingly* and voluntarily entered into this plea... these are facts learned after the plea, and I anticipate her testifying she would not have entered a plea accordingly."

Mortensen's arguments were stunningly accurate but did little to dissuade Caputo from his original stance, which Caputo firmly asserted despite the new evidence: "With respect to these documents and this additional evidence as you are arguing and previous to the argument, I reviewed the statute that the charges were amended from Murder in the Second Degree to Child Neglect. I don't see anything in the statue that has anything to do with causation. It has to do with her neglecting to supervise that eventually lead to the death of these children. So I don't see that any of this has any relevance to her withdrawing her plea. With respect to your comment about the factual basis of which she entered her plea having to deal with causation, causation isn't an element... It doesn't say anything about her responsibility to have started the fire. It says, very succinctly, the last two lines, "*I was neglectful and should not have left them.*"

Caputo's statement that causation was "not an element" was jaw-dropping to Chrisandria, sitting wide-eyed in the gallery. Isn't this what felony child neglect was predicated on? *Causing* the death of a child?

Caputo's retort brought Mortensen back to his original point. "I think what's important in this hearing, however, is what's in the mind of the defendant. And why did she enter a plea? And would she have entered a plea having now learned of new facts after her plea that would have materially changed her agreement to begin with?... These were facts learned *after the plea*... She also doesn't state in her factual basis on the plea form that the cause of the death necessarily was a lack of supervision. *You don't see supervision in that form!*"

McAmis interrupted, reiterating to Caputo her argument that the legal allowance for a plea withdrawal somehow didn't apply to this case. "Your Honor," she said. "Just because I don't want the record to be silent on this issue, I agree with Your Honor's ruling that this should not have any—this isn't relevant for the purposes of this hearing."

McAmis, a seasoned Assistant DA, was a fierce prosecutor of anyone remotely accused of child neglect. The purpose of the hearing, according to McAmis, was to lay guilt. It was her job—and she was good at it.

Caputo, for his part, typically nodded and yielded to her arguments.

27

The unanswered question

IN the absence of necessary witnesses to prove his argument, Mortensen called the only available person who could attest to the fundamental fact that Miashah was unaware of the new evidence: her former attorney, Fred DeMier.

Mortensen asked the judge for permission to put DeMier on the stand for questioning as to Miashah's reasoning in accepting a guilty plea in the first place. "As we're well aware, in this court as well as any other court, there are various factors that might lead one to enter into a plea agreement: a fear of jury trial, number one; a fear of the number of years that one might get; and the fear of certain issues with culpability. The culpability here I think is one of the prevailing issues in this case, and that is what I'm trying to address."

"And none of those have anything to do with the causation of the fire," Caputo stated, as if to ensure the futility of Mortensen's argument before he even began.

Under the weight of this edict—and Miashah's denouncement of his "inadequate counsel"—DeMier took the stand.

Mortensen began, "Okay, it says in this Motion to Withdraw Guilty Plea, filed on May 9, 2016, this motion was based on the fact that the plea was not 'knowingly' made because the attorney for the defendant did not sufficiently advise the defendant. What do you base this on, sir?"

DeMier responded, "Based on the conversation with my client saying that… there were outside factors that she had discovered since she entered her plea that she didn't know about at that time."

Mortensen continued, "And could you describe for us, briefly, as briefly as you could, what did this mean? What was she talking about?"

"She told me that she thought she should not be held responsible for the death of her nieces because of a case out of Mayes County where a woman who was on an ATV, driving while intoxicated and her two-year-old was killed, and she got released with a mere suspended sentence. She didn't understand why she couldn't have a suspended sentence. And she told me that she thought she had made a mistake and she wanted to go forward with the trial because of her religious beliefs that God would take care of her."

"Okay. Sir, did any of those discussions involve the documents that I showed you of the origin of the fire or electrical fires or any event?"

"Well, the documents that you showed me, *I knew about these allegations and ideas for several months, that that should probably be a part of the defense if we went to trial*—that that might be part of the defense and the jury would have to believe those documents, and that the State of Oklahoma would have to counter-argue against those, and we're not just going to walk in and present these documents and that would be it."

"Did you, in relation to these documents and that discussion, during the course of this case, did you retain an expert to—in regard to this defense?"

McAmis: "Objection to the relevance, Your Honor."

Judge Caputo: "Sustained."

Mortensen: "Judge, I'll pass the witness."

It was McAmis' turn to cross-examine the witness. She asked, "Did you, in fact, advise this defendant of your opinion when she approached you with her request to withdraw the plea?"

DeMier: "Yes, I did. I told her that I thought it would be a mistake.

McAmis: "Did you go over each of the questions on the [plea agreement] with the defendant before such time as she entered the plea?

DeMier: "Yes, I did, right in the jury box… I advised her we had to say she was neglectful to apply to the statute before I would take her plea."

McAmis: "And, of course, as you are aware in a Lumpkin [plea] form, there are answers that are circled to each of the questions. Did you go over the defendant's answers, and did she approve of the answers that you circled on the form?"

DeMier: "I went over it with her and told her what I had to—what I had to write in there had to comply with the statute saying she was pleading guilty of violating that statute and the neglect was the entire statute, basically."

McAmis: "And she approved of what you wrote in as the factual basis?"

DeMier: "Yes."

After quizzing DeMier further, she concluded her questioning.

Mortensen then asked permission for re-direct of DeMier.

"Can you briefly describe for the Court, as we've gone through this knowingly and voluntarily waiver, based on the facts of this case, *what discovery you had in your possession that you advised your client on in relation to the plea?*"

The question was pivotal to his argument that Miashah was unaware of the dangerous electrical problems at the complex, specifically in her unit—information DeMier had in his possession for over a year. Before DeMier could answer, McAmis objected again, reiterating to the judge that Miashah had "knowingly and voluntarily entered into that plea bargain."

Caputo once again sustained McAmis' objection and the question went unanswered.

Mortensen then pressed the issue of exactly what evidence Miashah had become aware of after her guilty plea that caused her to rethink her decision as to her own culpability in the death of the children, specifically about other factors that may have caused the fire.

Mortensen: "Do you understand that to be a basis for her request to withdraw her plea?"

DeMier: "Yes."

Mortensen: "You do!?"

DeMier: "I understand that she feels like she wasn't neglectful, and at this point I discussed that with her thoroughly."

Mortensen: "But you would agree with me that that was a part of the discussion and a part of her reason why she wants to withdraw the plea?"

DeMier: "We did discuss the fact that she had changed her mind and wanted to withdraw her plea because she felt she really didn't understand everything."

DeMier had just stated for the Court that there were material facts he had not made Miashah aware of: engineering reports and explicit input given to him by Tankersley and Palau describing the dangerous electrical conditions in the complex. A key tenant of the statute for plea withdrawal is whether the plea was "knowingly and voluntarily" entered." The definition of knowingly is "fully aware." The new evidence would have materially affected her decision to accept the DA's guilty plea for something she had nothing to do with and could easily have led any safety-conscious juror to conclude "reasonable doubt" as to exactly who was responsible—Miashah or London Square. DeMier had withheld evidence germane to the very crux of her plea agreement.

"I have no further questions," Mortensen said. DeMier was excused from the stand.

Mortensen then spoke directly to the judge. "I believe, after having a discussion with Ms. Moses, the defendant in this case, after talking with Mr. DeMier, after reviewing the documents that I've handed the Court—exhibits 1 through 10—I believe that the defendant would testify that, in fact, she felt responsible for setting the fire and that she believed that was a large part of what this case was about was starting a fire and leaving. And, so, as I stated before, her understanding of what the charge is and what the facts are is of central important to this case. And, really, the only thing of any importance or relevance in a motion to withdraw a plea is her understanding, and more importantly, if this would have had a material impact on her decision to enter a plea."

After further arguments to the Court and repeated objections by McAmis, all of which were sustained by Judge Caputo, Mortensen concluded with a heartfelt plea. "Judge, at the end of the day, I'm not—again, I'm not asking for the Court to excuse her or for the State to give her a better deal. I'm not asking for any of that stuff. Here's what I'm asking: That she be allowed that fundamental right that everyone of us should enjoy, and that is simply, let's go before a jury to present those facts that were not known to her, to a jury… and let them decide the degree of her culpability in this matter. That's the only request that I'm asking before you today and ask that you follow that and allow her an opportunity to request a jury trial at the Court's earliest convenience."

Caputo leaned forward and dug in. "It's evidence that was discovered during the pendency of this trial and was discussed between Mr. DeMier and his client… Maybe the documents might be newly discovered, but the facts at issue are not newly discovered… she offered her plea knowingly, willfully and voluntarily in this matter."

Chrisandria and family members sat in the gallery bewildered. What seemed to escape the judge's attention was that, due to McAmis' earlier objections, DeMier had never been allowed to answer Mortensen's question as to whether he had actually shown the evidence to or discussed it with Miashah. How could she have "knowingly" entered into a plea agreement for 15 years in prison if she didn't know the evidence existed? Emails from Tankersley and Palau had arrived after her guilty plea and were Miashah's first real clues that electrical deficiencies might have started the fire. Nor had she seen Tankersley's detailed reports from a licensed electrician pointing to the overloaded circuits and frayed wiring as the probable cause of the fire.

It was to no avail. Caputo turned and fixed his eyes on Miashah. "Ms. Moses, in this Court and as, hopefully, in all of the Courts, there is no such thing as "mulligans" or "buyer's remorse." *You get one shot at a plea.* And if it's done without any coercion, without any promise, without any undue pressure, influence or duress... it is accepted by the Courts."

The gist of the hearing that day was captured in a brief excerpt from the June 17, 2015, online case docket:

> DEFENDANT'S ORAL REQUEST FOR CONTINUANCE IS DENIED. DEFENDANT'S ORAL REQUEST TO AMEND ORDER TO WITHDRAW PLEA TO SHOW NEWLY DISCOVERY EVIDENCE IS DENIED. MOTION TO WITHDRAW PLEA IS DENIED.

*

On June 3, 2016, Mortensen filed a notice of intent to appeal Caputo's decision with the Oklahoma Court of Criminal Appeals titled, "Advisory Proposition for Error." It cited three basic areas in which Caputo's denial for a plea withdrawal ignored the basic rules of allowance:

1. The Trial Court erred by denying new counsel the ability to amend the Motion to Withdraw Plea to include a claim of newly discovered evidence;
2. The Trial Court erred by not allowing the Motion to Withdraw Plea;
3. The Trial Court erred by denying the Defendant the ability to present evidence regarding her claim of newly discov-

ered evidence, and took as fact an alternative reason for the Defendants reason to withdraw a plea.

In short, judges should not substitute their own "alternative reason" for allowing or denying a legally allowable plea withdrawal when new and relevant facts are discovered that would have materially affected the Defendant's original pleading.[74] This is precisely why newly discovered evidence causes convictions to be overturned every day in the United States.

As for other outside evidence that might have aided in exonerating Miashah, there was another matter. While Fred DeMier had asked the Court for a delay in the jury trial nearly one year earlier in order to locate an expert forensic witness, he had never actually done so. Chrisandria, on the other hand had contacted Dr. Gerald Hurst, a pro-bono expert forensic fire investigator from Texas with notoriety for reversing judgments in lethal fire cases where children had died. One of them involved Terri Henson, a defendant on death row.

Hurst had succeeded in freeing Henson, a young single mother in North Carolina accused of murder in a case eerily similar to Miashah's. In November, 1996, a fire burned down Hinson's house, killing her 1-year-old son Joshua. Hinson escaped with her six-year-old daughter, but she was unable to save Joshua, who was sitting in a bouncer in an upstairs bedroom. Police accused Terri of setting the fire herself by cooking on the stove. Authorities took away her daughter and put her in a foster home, and Terri was charged with first-degree murder.

Put under house arrest, she bought a computer and logged onto the Internet. By searching the Web, she came across Dr. Hurst, who agreed to take her case pro bono. Hurst found evidence of electrical malfunction in a floor heater: overloaded, underpowered circuitry in a home with 50-year-old wiring originally designed for 15 amps that was wired to a 30-amp fuse box that had blown. "That means you're carrying more power to that wire than it was designed to carry," he said. In this case, that fragile wiring in the attic fed the 1500-watt oven. The heater, which had never been plugged in before, overloaded the circuit. As the line eroded, the overheated electrical wires arced, and sparks contacted the grease trap over the oven. "Coils don't conduct electricity," he said, "but grease does." A wooden ceiling and a jump-started fire caused a holocaust in no time at all.

Hurst believed that local fire officials had rushed to judgement. Fire investigators long worked from a basic set of assumptions about how buildings burn. "Old wives' tales," Hurst called them. He sent the prosecutor his critique of the investigation, which stated that their conclusion was based on "junk science," essentially confusing the actual cause of the fire, frayed wiring, with the end result of the fire, which they wrongfully deduced was a hot stove.

The Court agreed with Hurst's findings that faulty electrical wiring caused the fire. The murder charge was dropped against Terry Henson, but she had already lost her home and her child because of an inaccurate conclusion drawn from faulty science. "Fire investigation in general is the swamp of forensic science," Hurst said.

Hurst was widely known to work pro bono on those cases he deemed worthy. Hearing Chrisandria's pleas, in late 2014 Hurst agreed to analyze the ATF and fire investigators' reports in Miashah's case. To do so, he needed copies of all available fire reports. Chrisandria tried in vain to obtain the ATF fire reports that DeMier's partner, Charles Reese, said proved the fire was electrical. But DeMier refused, saying Miashah was his client, not Chrisandria. In essence, he cut off

Chrisandria and the family from pursuing any outside analysis on their own for Miashah's defense.

Hurst died of complications from a liver transplant the following year, still awaiting critical fire and ATF data that could have exonerated Miashah. Regardless, in view of Judge Caputo's impregnable stance as to causation, Chrisandria was doubtful that even an industry expert such as Hurst could have changed his mind.

It was later discovered that the portion of Miashah's guilty plea acknowledging that she "knowingly and voluntarily" entered the plea was never completed. The entire section was blank. Directly below was the signature of Judge James W. Caputo.

In the five minutes she was given to review the 130-plus lines of fine print, sixty scribbled entries by DeMier, and thirty-nine items circled "yes" or "no," was it pointed out to her that on item 37.C she was admitting to have "knowingly and willingly" left the children to die?—or was that lost in the rush.

THE COURT FINDS AS FOLLOWS:

37. A. The Defendant was sworn and responded to questions under oath.

B. The Defendant understands the nature, purpose and consequences of this proceeding.

C. The Defendant's plea(s) of ______________________ is/are knowingly and voluntarily entered and accepted by the Court.

D. The Defendant is competent for the purpose of this hearing.

E. A factual basis exists for the plea(s) (and former conviction(s), if applicable).

F. The Defendant is guilty as charged: (check as appropriate)

( ) after no prior felony convictions.

( ) after one (1) prior felony conviction.

( ) after two (2) or more prior felony convictions.

G. Sentencing or order deferring sentence shall be: imposed instanter ( ); or continued until the ______ day of ____________, 20 ___, at ______ ___.m.

If the Pre-Sentence Investigation and Report is requested, it shall be provided to the Court by the ______ day of ____________, 20 ___.

H. Defendant is committed to:

____ The RID Program

____ The FORT Program

____ The Delayed Sentencing Program for Youthful Offenders

DONE IN OPEN COURT this ~~18~~ 27 day of April, 20 16

[signature]
Court Reporter Present

[signature]
JUDGE OF THE DISTRICT COURT

[signature]
Deputy Court Clerk

____
NAME OF JUDGE TYPED OR PRINTED

Form 4058 (Rev. 2-15)

5

28

Lost in intolerance

WHEN he assumed the role of DA in 2015 with some fifty prosecutors reporting to him, Kunzweiler had already spent 25 years under the protection of a powerful state prosecutorial agency. His entire career was filtered through the harsh lens of prosecution shielded with impunity. As in most states, Oklahoma tax dollars pay for judges and district attorneys who prosecute the most vulnerable citizens. They not only get paid for being right, they get paid even when they're wrong. Not justice for all, only justice for some. If you're the right color with respectable looks and money, you might receive a more lenient sentence, possibly an outright dismissal.

Such bending of justice occurred more than once under Judge Caputo's reign in power. The most notable was a 2010 triple manslaughter case against Steve Jameson, a clean-cut 19-year-old, in a head-on crash that killed three family members—a husband, a wife, and their 18-year-old son. Jameson, who was white, was driving "in a reckless manner" while speeding. He filed a blind guilty plea, but then changed his mind. Caputo allowed Jameson to withdraw his blind guilty plea, and he was released on bond. The Oklahoma Court of Criminal Appeals disagreed with Caputo's decision. Justices in the appellate court ruled that Caputo had acted improperly. The reversal was the third opinion in Jameson's case that ordered a reversal of a decision made by Caputo. After the resounding legal defeats, Caputo reluctantly recused himself.

In another case, 26-year-old John Freeman, who was white, pled guilty to a DUI manslaughter charge and was sentenced by Judge Caputo to life in prison. Freeman had a blood-alcohol level nearly three times the legal limit and admitted he was driving drunk and going the wrong way when he crashed head-on into a car driven by 64-year-old O. Z. Walker, a black man, killing him instantly. A year later, Caputo reduced Freeman's sentence from life to only five years after Freeman's attorney described him as "a perfect example of a good person making a horrible lapse in judgment."

Meanwhile, Miashah, a diminutive black girl of little means, requested a plea withdrawal based on newly discovered evidence and was roundly chastised by Caputo for "knowingly and willingly" pleading guilty.

Entering Judge Caputo's courtroom appeared to be a game of judicial roulette whose outcome depended on your connections, ethnicity, and legal posture.[75]

*

On June 20, 2016, at a back booth in a Tulsa restaurant, Chrisandria met with two documentary filmmakers from New York and California, both females. One was a minority who represented a women's defense group in New York, and the other was an award-winning member of a feature documentary team with the Sundance Film Festival, curating and discovering U.S. and international documentaries. They made the trip to Tulsa that week to research the reasons behind Oklahoma's high rate of female incarceration, the highest in the country. The notoriety of Miashah's case had caught their attention.

"It's a slow brainwashing," Chrisandria said, describing the way things work in the Oklahoma justice system. "You see a chicken, and they tell you it's a duck."

"'But it looks like a chicken!' you say. 'No, it's a duck,' they insist. They keep telling you it's a duck, until you finally start thinking, 'Well, maybe *it is* a duck…' The next thing you know, you're on your way to prison."

"Black people have a saying about Oklahoma," she said. "*Come on vacation, leave on probation.*"

The conversation left the documentalists, one a minority, struck with the racial disparities that could be looming in the streets of Tulsa. As they left the restaurant later that evening, they looked around the parking lot and voiced concern about being pulled over by the police on their drive back to the hotel. With Miashah's outlook as a potential inmate at one of the state's largest women's prison, Mabel Bassett, the documentarians intended to focus on this minimum-maximum security prison, among others, as potential sites for filming.

The film makers planned to feature Mabel Bassett in the film by way of access to a handful of inmates in the prison. Multiple requests for access to prison inmates to Mabel Bassett's warden, the head of Oklahoma Department of Corrections, and other industry contacts were stonewalled. Finally, after exhausting all available means of gaining access to inmates at Mabel Bassett, they gave up. They gave up just like the many of the inmates had done when jailed guilty. In the face of insurmountable institutional opposition, they gave up.

With the final link in the justice chain now severed, Miashah's journey was destined to follow the path of many others: an initial flash of publicity and legal analysis followed by a slow fading from the collective memory, finally receding into the files of innumerable other questionable cases. Another woman scuttled to prison. Another statistic in Oklahoma's growing female inmate population.

"There is no peace if the Devil's got you wrapped up in anger," Miashah said. "It's time to let God be God."

PART 3

LOCKED UP

Not all things are as they seem.

29

The road to prison

"It's time to pull chains!"

The detention officer's voice echoed through Pod F-20 at 2:30 a.m. on May 25, 2016. It was the clarion call to rouse inmates for "chaining up." Miashah knew it would happen—she just didn't know when.

It was dead of night when guards harnessed her in belly chains and loaded her into a van chained to a half-dozen other women, all naked beneath their orange jump suits. No bras. No underwear. Those had to be left behind.

"It was pitch black, I had no idea where I was or where I was going," she said.

The driver pulled out of the David L. Moss County Jail and headed west on I-44. An hour later, headlights peered down exit 158 for McCloud, Oklahoma. The van veered to the right down a series of ever-narrowing country roads, finally emerging at a stop sign on Broadway Street next to the McCloud Country Café, a local favorite as old as the town itself. The diner was the last sign of civilization inmates would see for months, maybe years, maybe ever. A short ride west on Broadway, and the van slowed at small green arrow in the weeds labeled "Cemetery," an ironic marker toward the tomb of the living dead. The driver took a hard-right turn at the arrow and the landscape lapsed into total obscurity, winding down gravel roads past bales of hay and farmhouses, an occasional porchlight offering the only evidence of human life in the darkness.

Nine miles down the road, the bulging razor wire atop the 12-foot fence loomed in the distance around Mabel Bassett Women's Correctional Center, a dimly lit, sprawling gray concrete structure squatted in the middle of nowhere, a barren, frightening place.

Chains rattled as the inmates exited the van single-file to enter what is arguably a state-sanctioned warehouse for the living dead. Over the next 30-days they would be evaluated by prison staff to determine their ultimate destination. Some stay at Mabel Bassett. Others are sent to one of six other women's prisons across the state, each stuffed to the maximum with women of all ages and races. There was the 31-year-old woman accused of allowing her father to abuse her four-year-old daughter[76]; the 70-year-old gray-haired grandmother sentenced to life in prison for shooting her ex-husband twice in the head, allegedly in self-defense[77]; and the 25-year-old Hispanic mother of four sentenced to 10 years for selling $31 worth of marijuana to an undercover cop.[78]

And, of course, there was Miashah.

Prison-issue attire at Mabel Bassett consists of a drab, gray V-neck shirt, matching baggy pants, a single pair of underpants, and a bra. For inmates with urinary incontinence or menstrual issues, things can get messy. With no outside support or funds in their commissary accounts to buy more underwear, things get even messier. Some girls craft tampons of paper towels and toilet paper; that is, if they have any toilet paper left. Inmates are issued one role of toilet paper per week. Lisa, a 52-year-old inmate serving eight years for forging a prescription for a controlled prescription drug, begged a member of a visiting church group to please see if she could get a fresh pair of underwear, priced at $10 on the commissary list. Common necessities in the outside world are luxuries at Mabel Bassett. Girls can get killed over them.

The prison houses women in medium- and maximum-security wings where inmates share a common prison yard. Housing is also available for prisoners with specialized physical or mental health needs. Inmates say that even if a woman doesn't need mental health care when she arrives at Mabel Bassett, she likely will before she leaves.

It isn't only prisoners who suffer rough treatment at Mabel Bassett. Visitors are often treated as subhuman as well. That is, if they're able to find the prison in the first place.

The prison is located on a large section of sparse land in the middle of central Oklahoma, "where the wind comes sweeping down the plains." The main building is barely visible from the closest asphalt road. Even when visitors find it, they might not know it. Many inmates' families lack reliable transportation to make the drive to the prison, and there is no public transportation to or from the prison.

If visitors do finally find the prison, challenges await. Outside the entrance, visitors shuffle through two enormous electric sliding gates programmed to never be open at the same time. It's not uncommon for visitors to stand outside in the weather for half an hour waiting for gates to be activated by prison guards monitoring them from the admitting area inside. Once inside the building, more rules are added.

Visitors are permitted visitation only on specific days of the week based on the first letter of the inmate's last name. "M" visitors, for inmates like Miashah Moses, for example, are permitted only on Sundays. Visits are not to exceed one hour and visitors must undergo a background check 90 days in advance. Anyone with the hint of a shady background is denied. Some are denied for no specified reason. Visitors who show up on the wrong day are intercepted by a prison guard and turned around for a long ride back home. Those arriving from out of state could be in for a rude awakening.

Visitors' attire is restricted, and the wrong choice of clothes can result in a denied visitation. Sleeveless, gray, black, or periwinkle-blue shirts are prohibited, as are hats, leggings, shorts, or shoes without backs. All jewelry except wedding rings must be removed, including body piercings, which can be embarrassing for visitors with piercings in private places. Shoes must be removed so that the bottoms of visitors' feet can be checked visually for hidden items. The restricted clothing sign shown outside the prison does not match the list posted on the Mabel Bassett website, so regular visitors bring multiple changes of clothes in their car. First-time visitors often retreat to the McCloud Walmart to buy acceptable attire. One young woman with a baby found it especially unpleasant.

She said, "They make it so hard for people to visit. Every little thing. For the first two or three times I went there I had to go out to my car to take something back. Two or three times. 'You can't wear this—you can't wear…' I mean, I understand a dress code, but, I mean, certain things in the baby's diaper bag, like he had a diaper rash. I couldn't take in his diaper cream but I couldn't go out to get it to change his diaper, because my visit would be, you know, terminated. And, it was just one thing after another. The guards hassle you—constantly."[79]

Once finally cleared, visitors shuffle to a nearby desk where IDs are computer-checked for authorized visitation. Visitors are then directed by a guard to walk through a dual-sided metal detector. Visitors who activate alarms are body-scanned by a second guard. Anyone suspected of carrying contraband is subject to a strip search or sniffed by drug dogs for hidden stashes.

Once past security, a prison guard presses a button to release a thick gray steel door, admitting visitors into a small chamber, roughly six feet square, with yet another locked steel door on the opposite side. The ominous ratcheting of bolts can be heard as the first door locks behind them, securing the captors in the chamber. A one-way mirror at one end obscures guards, who monitor the small room until all are inside. Then, with the push of a button, locks of the second door snap open, releasing visitors into a large room resembling a gymnasium, revealing a scatter of 28 round tables, benches, and folding chairs.

The noise level reaches a circus-like crescendo as gray-clad inmates stream into the room from a door at the back and are greeted by excited family and friends. Kids run gleefully into their mother's arms, and inmates cry as they hug their children.

A row of canteens line the corner of a back wall. A thick green line painted on the floor several feet in front marks the demarcation inmates are not allowed to cross. Only prison personnel and visitors can access vending machines. Inmates watch from behind the green line, motioning for drinks, cookies, snacks, and sandwiches—anything tastier than the usual prison food. Visitors can be rare for many of the thousand-plus inmates. Lack of time, money, or simply caring—or perhaps the incredibly tedious visitor application process has dwindled their hopes.

For the first three years she was incarcerated at Mabel Bassett, no Moses family member visited Miashah. Chrisandria did her best to visit her daughter, but her visitation application was denied repeatedly for different reasons. Even a birthday card she mailed was returned undelivered. The prison form enclosed said it "contained glitter." The sparkly substance, she learned, was considered "contraband" by prison officials, a potentially dangerous object. So were staples and tape to hold letters together and a book of stamps that might contain amphetamines in the adhesive.

Her brother Keontae applied to visit, but he was denied for using an outdated form and failing to properly complete the required blanks. The online visitor form is confusing, unforgiving, and constantly changing, sometimes in the small print. This means that the last one used may not be valid for another attempt. A prospective visitor might submit a corrected application on the same form, only to have it denied again because it is no longer on the correct form.

The troubling problem for Miashah was that she had no shoes, and inmates are prohibited from receiving packages from family and friends. Inmates are provided only flimsy orange slip-ons, dubbed "Gilligans," with no backs or means of securing them on her feet. Like most of her fellow inmates, she has no money in her account to buy shoes through the prison commissary. She has a passion for basketball and grew up shooting baskets with her little brother, Jacquen, as a kid, and in spite of her 5'2" height, she was good at it. Outdoor basketball courts are available, weather permitting, but it's hard to dribble in flip-flops, so she plays basketball in borrowed tennis shoes.

She works in the kitchen for the state pay of 80 cents an hour, balancing her short stature on a stool to stir large pots that frequently splash boiling soup on her arms. During the prison's initial orientation, each inmate is given a small plastic kit containing essentials: toothpaste, a toothbrush, soap, and female hygiene products. If she loses anything, she's on their own. Detention officers are generally unsympathetic.

Wendy, an inmate who arrived when Miashah did, learned this the hard way when she lost her one and only prison-issued toothbrush. "I just sat on the stairs and put my head in my arms and cried," she said. It was a small sample of the suffering yet to come.

How a small-town girl like Wendy came to be there was a saga of its own.

30

The wheels of injustice

WENDY'S journey from a small town of Bristow in the quiet backwoods of Oklahoma, to Mabel Bassett was unpredictable and ugly.

Her friends knew her as a spunky, blonde version of Rosie O'Donnell, with bright cheeks and a permanent grin. No prissy hidden agendas or phony table talk. If ever there was anyone who could excel at being herself, it was Wendy. Even the most miserable, rude people were no match for her happy comebacks. Insulting her was a waste of time. Her well-crafted retorts were always delivered with style and a smile. You couldn't help but like her, but you pity the poor guy who crosses her—which is what happened one late night in September, 2012.

She was 31 when she was arrested in her son's high school parking lot. She'd been driving around town with her boyfriend, who was in the passenger seat, when a heated argument broke out. He wanted her to take him to a cell phone store. She refused. They argued. Suddenly he pulled out a knife and lunged at her, stabbing her in the side. Enraged, she hit the gas pedal and sped through town and slammed on the brakes at a stop sign. The passenger door flew open and she kicked him out. "He was ready to get out, and I helped him," she said.

Two hours later she was still mad that he got away with it. Not the kind of woman to let a man get the last word, she dug a .40-caliber pistol out of the dresser and headed to his house in her son's long-bed pickup, loading the pistol on the way. When she got there, she could hear him talking inside, but he wouldn't answer the door. Furious, she stood on the porch and fired the gun in the air several times. She then hopped back in the truck, stuffed the gun in a camera case, threw it in the back seat, and drove home.

The next day, her son and his friend drove the truck to a high school football practice. After practice, the friend was fooling around in the back seat and found it. Neither knew how it got there, so they went back inside the school and told the coach. He called the police and they confiscated the gun and the truck.

Rather than have her son arrested for harboring a weapon, Wendy turned herself in at the Creek County Sheriff's Office. Possession of a gun is sacred and legal in Oklahoma, but Wendy's gun was in the back seat of a truck on school property, which is *not* legal.

DA Max Cook was the undisputed czar of the Creek County Criminal Justice Center and was known for his predilection for meeting out whip-saw judgments that pushed the pushed the maximums of law. Grudges in the Creek County Criminal Justice Center could last a lifetime. Its reputation was well known in surrounding jurisdictions, as was attested to when an abused Tulsa woman asked a Tulsa police sharpshooter if he knew what happened to her ex-husband. "I hear he's buried in a shallow grave in Creek County," he quipped.

Wendy was about to get a first-hand taste of Creek County justice. "Creek County is the worst of the worst," she said."If there were too many girls, some had to sleep on the floor," she said. "At one point, we had 'under-the-stair girls' because they slept on a matt underneath the stairs."

When prisoners are first admitted to the Creek County Jail, they undergo a mandatory screening. "A nurse asked me if I ever had suicidal thoughts. And I said 'Well, haven't we all? But nobody ever has the balls to do it!'"

This flippant response got Wendy put on suicide watch. "That's the worst thing you can be on in Creek County," she said. "When they bring you in, they're looking for reasons to fight with you."

She was put in a green cloth outfit with Velcro straps called a "turtle suit." "It was scratchy, it was horrible. You get no matt and you get no pillow. And you have to sleep on the floor for the first 24 hours. No shower for four days. Nothing. No socks or shoes, and you're freezing to death," she said. "And you have no underwear underneath cause they're afraid you might hang yourself with it or something."

They left the lights on 24 hours a day. For five days she was locked in a small pod outside the guard area until she could be evaluated by a psychiatrist who came in once a week. It was humiliating. "They have cameras on you all the time," she said. "There's nothing but men watching you, so when you had to go to the bathroom you had to hike it up while they watched." She begged to call her mother, to call her attorney, to call anybody, but the guards mocked her, saying "We can't he-e-e-a-r you!"

The psychiatrist finally came and said there was nothing wrong with her, and guards moved her to a standard jail cell. "The whole environment was horrible," she said. "They would only let me outside one day a week—a caged yard in the middle of the jail. Walls all around."

She finally got an attorney and went to court. She was put on probation and given a five-year suspended sentence for unlawful possession of a weapon on school property. But the DA was still mad that she got out of the weapon charge. "He thought I was cocky. They were looking' for a reason to take me."

On August 17, 2014, they found a reason. It was a Sunday morning when they busted through her kitchen door, handcuffs in tow. "I had the garage door wide open," she said. "It wasn't like I was trying to hide anything."

They came straight through the garage and pounded on the door. They yelled, "We're coming in. We have a warrant!" Wendy had bought a washer and dryer on Craigslist from a girl who said she was leaving town and needed to sell everything. The washer was too big for the space, so she left it in the garage and posted it back on Craigslist. It turned out the washer and dryer were stolen. The original owner spotted the listing and called the police. "I explained the situation to them. I even had a receipt!" Wendy said. But they handcuffed her anyway and took her to jail. It was an ugly ride.

She kept telling them they're crazy for taking her in for that. "I was mad and yelling at them," she said. "Finally, the officer in front seat turned around and said, 'I'm going to shove my dick in your mouth if you don't shut up!'"

"Really?" she answered. "You're going to stick your dick in my mouth? I'm ready! Do it!"

"They were horrible. They were horrible, horrible people," she said. "I still have nightmares about that ride."

She fought the charge for two years, until her attorney bumped his head and developed amnesia. "Seriously. He had no recollection of the case or that I'd even paid him any money. He almost died."

With only nine months left in her five-year probation on the earlier gun charge, Creek County DA Max Cook dropped the gavel on her Craigslist charge. Now in violation of her probation, she was sentenced to two years of state incarceration.

In the early morning hours of June 21, 2016, she took the same van ride to Mabel Bassett that Miashah had taken four months earlier.

As with all inmates, Wendy was placed in a large pod with other women to be evaluated. Some of the women she arrived with were transferred to minimum security prisons. Others stayed at Mabel Bassett. No matter where they were headed, each inmate was put in 23-hour lockdown for ten to 30 days. They ate, showered, and made phone calls from one common area. For 24 hours a day, when she wasn't sleeping, she watched out a small window to see what was going on in the yard.

"There's no question where they get meth," she said. "They get it in the yard. I saw a drone coming in and drop something and go out. I was mesmerized. How was I the only one who saw that? I mean, it was crazy!"

There were fights and all kinds of things going on in that yard. It took the guards a few minutes to break it up, but if somebody had a weapon, it doesn't take long to get pretty beat up—like a 'lock in a sock.' One pop with one of those, and I've seen girls with boulder-size lumps on their head," she said. "I've never seen anyone else get beat up that bad."

She said on her third day at Mabel Bassett, a nurse had given an inmate the wrong medication. As she was walking back to her pod, the inmate collapsed and died on the stairs. "I think they reported that she bumped her head in transportation," Wendy said.

"Every day I was there, I saw an ambulance. Every day."

After being held 17 days at Mabel Bassett, Wendy was deemed a minimum-security risk and transferred to Kate Bernard Correctional Center, a minimum-security prison in Oklahoma City. She was released two months later. "I did a 90-day turnaround," she smiled.

Upon release, she took a job waitressing at a small Tulsa midtown diner, arriving at 5:00 a.m. to prep the tables and open the doors at 6:00. Customers arriving at the diner for early morning coffee had no idea a convicted felon was taking their order.

Nor did Wendy know that her fellow waitress, Jeannie, had been down the same road.

31

Roped and tied

JEANNIE was not cut out to be a waitress.

The whip-smart 23-year-old didn't need a college education to figure out the basic things a girl needs in life, or how to bite a bullet when things didn't go her way. She came from a conservative family that could never quite fathom her rebellious spirit. Her father, in particular, tried futilely to manage his blue-eyed baby girl, but she grew into a full-blown woman of the same rebellious nature she'd had as a girl. And although her mother loved her dearly, she gave up trying to corral her daughter long ago. The only corral Jeannie wanted was on a ranch in the Wild West with a cowboy.

What she didn't know was that a woman's chance of landing in jail in Oklahoma's Wild West is almost three times higher than any other state.[80] And it doesn't take much. If you're in the wrong place at the wrong time, the sticky fingers of the law will suck you in like a Venus fly trap. Flashing red lights can appear in the rear-view mirror out of nowhere.

Such was the case for Jeannie in the early morning hours on March 14, 2018.

It happened outside a west Tulsa Waffle House where she and her good friend Joey were chowing down after an evening at Westbound, a favorite hangout of country-western fans. The bar was located two miles west of the Arkansas River, a winding waterway that separated elite midtown Tulsa County residents on the east side of the river from their less-sophisticated Tulsa neighbors on the west. The club is one of the few places in town with a dance floor and live country music. The music is loud and the place is smoky, but the drinks are cheap. Neon lights flashed and pool tables rattle with racked balls. Ladies night meant longnecks for a buck.

The petite redhead had a feisty attitude that made her irresistible to boot-stomping cowboys at the popular western hot spot. Her controlling husband, however, didn't like her Westbound nights with the cowboys. Her grandmother had told her not to marry him. Jeannie had two special-needs daughters from a previous marriage, ages 6 and 7, the older one autistic, and the younger on the spectrum. But she was 26 and in love. She married him despite the warnings.

"Three days after the wedding," she said, "he flipped a switch."

Behind closed doors, he grew violent, beating Jeannie and her daughters with his hands, with a belt, with anything he could find. Once, he dislocated her shoulder. Another time he cracked two of her ribs. The oldest daughter suffered a concussion. He wouldn't allow Jeannie to go online or use the phone or talk to her family. She managed to separate from him for a short time, but the separation only made him angrier. He accused her of having an affair and set out to punish her for perceived transgressions. He said his mafia friends in Chicago had told him he had to do it, but he was always making things up.

"So, he goes and gets a bottle of Vida, gauze, Neosporin, and he's got, like, this Samurai sword," she said. He put the sword in a pot of boiling water for an hour or more, then stripped her naked, taped up her hands and feet, forced her onto her knees, and asked her if she wanted something to bite down on because "this is going to hurt."

"Just do it," she told him.

He came back with the hot sword, planning to brand her with the letter 'A' on her butt—the scarlet letter. But he chickened out. He barely touched her skin, and pulled away, saying something was telling him not to go through with it.

That's when she decided to get out. By the time she filed the report, she was covered in bruises. "The female officer at the precinct got really mad," Jeannie said. "She filed assault and battery and child abuse charges against him and took pictures. He had hit me with my heavy metal purse and left a dent in my head where he smacked it." But a male detective told her they couldn't really do anything unless they caught him in the act, because the court system would never believe her.

She finally got out of the terrible marriage. Newly divorced, she landed a job at a Tulsa recycling plant. But the job was only part-time and barely covered her $600 rent. There weren't many good times to be had, so she was glad when Joey called and asked if she could meet him at Westbound. Friends at the bar sent over a couple of rounds of drinks to the table. The band "Johnny Duke and Shootout" was playing. The dance floor was hopping. Life was good.

At 2:00 a.m. closing time, they headed to the nearby Waffle House on I-44 for food to soak up the beer and shots. They couldn't have picked a worse place. The Waffle House was in Creek County.

She saw the police cruiser when she pulled into the restaurant but didn't think the cops would still be there when she left. She sat inside for an hour, visiting with Joey over a plate of steak and eggs. It was when she pulled out of the parking lot in her beat-up car that they spotted her. She couldn't afford much of a car after the divorce, so she was driving a white 2008 Chevy Malibu she called the "one-eyed wonder" because it was missing a headlight. The police were parked down the street and pulled her over for that missing headlight. She rolled down her window and gave them her driver's license and insurance card.

"Ma'am, you need to get out of the car," the officer said.

"Why?" she asked.

"Seriously, I can smell the alcohol from here."

There were two cop cars behind him, four officers altogether. They ordered her to put her hands on the car and patted her down. They made her walk, touch her nose, and shined a light in her eyes to check dilation.

"You failed the sobriety test and you're under arrest for DUI," the officer said.

She was promptly stuck in the back of a cop car and driven to the police station. She was then driven straight to the Creek County Jail, where she sat in the booking area for nearly three hours.

"I was really tired. They gave me a blanket and I just passed out on a bench," she said. When she was finally taken to booking, they asked, "Are you having suicidal thoughts?"

She answered, "Well, yeah, you know, my life's over. I'm going to jail, these are serious charges, I may just hang myself." She was kidding, but there's no joking around in Creek County.

She could hear the girls in the back of the jail saying, "Don't say that… you don't want that turtle suit, girl! You don't want that turtle suit!"

"Strip," they said. "You're going on suicide watch."

"So I'm sitting there naked," she said. She was put on suicide watch. The turtle suit, the cold cell, the isolation, same as Wendy. "It had Velcro straps across the chest, across the waist, on both sides. It was like 30 degrees in my cell, and I started shaking really bad," she said. "So, I knocked on the door and said, 'Hey, can I have a blanket?'"

"No! You're on suicide watch, you can't get anything!" they said.

She woke up in the middle of the night, thirsty and scared. It was then she discovered the sink didn't work. She could hear guards talking and laughing down the hall, so she knocked on the door to get their attention.

They yelled, "Whadda you want!!"

"Can I have some water, please?"

"No!!"

"The sink in here doesn't work. Can I please have some water?"

"You should just drink out of the toilet then!"

So she went without water. The male detention officers leered at her through the ceiling cameras mounted in her cell. "There was a female on duty when I went in, but for the next four days all I heard were male voices," she said. She heard the men but couldn't see them. They covered up the one small window in her cell. They could see her through the camera, but she couldn't see them. She would bang on the door to get their attention, but that only made the guards angry. They called her names—bitch, cunt. They threatened her. She feared they would taser her or restrain her. She'd seen a man strapped into a chair the same way they strap down someone before killing them in an electric chair. Straps across the legs, the arms, the chest, the neck. She didn't want that. "He was tied down in the 'high-risk' room, and they'd just go in there and tase him for the fun of it."

She spent four days in the turtle suit until the psych doctor finally came on Monday morning. The doctor said she could be released. At that point, they gave her the kit with the toothbrush, toothpaste, and a bar of soap. There was no shampoo. If she wanted shampoo, she'd have to buy it from the commissary. She'd come into jail with $35 in cash, but they never logged it. She'd now been moved to the women's standard pod and was sleeping on the floor, because there were no bunks available.

They gave her a pair of slippers that rubbed blisters on her feet. "They were like ghetto shoes," she said. "They were the most ratty, broken-down shoes. They rubbed blisters, they stunk, and they don't clean 'em. A man could have worn 'em. A woman could have worn 'em. And they were hard. I got two left feet because that's all they had, and one of them was busted and held together by a rubber band." No socks. If she wanted socks, she'd have to buy those from the commissary too. Later, just before she was released, another woman was issued two right shoes in the same size, and Jeannie was able to trade one of her lefties. But the shoes were so hard and uncomfortable, it didn't make much difference.

After a month in the Creek County Jail, Joey finally found her and bailed her out. She went to court and pled guilty to driving under the influence. Now, in addition to the $600 rent she couldn't afford, she had nearly $5,000 in court costs and fines to pay off. At $50 a week, it would take her eight years to pay it off—maybe longer.

On her first night of freedom, she headed back to Westbound. Her friends smiled. "We know where you've been," they said. "What's it like in Creek County?"

Jeannie shrugged. "You need to be tough, or something bigger and badder is going to come along and treat you like roadkill."

Less than a year later, she walked out of her waitress job at the Tulsa diner and left town. She was last seen heading west with a cowboy.

*

32

Life interrupted

MIASHAH had been in prison only one month when she learned of another inmate from Tulsa with a prison sentence more egregious than her own. "There's a beautiful girl here," she said, somewhat in awe. "She's really pretty. She's here for an accident that killed her husband."

Amber Hilberling was a beauty, even in prison. Miashah first noticed her across the room in the visitor's area where Amber spent time with her 5-year-old son, Levi. She had been there almost three years when Miashah arrived.

Amber Hilberling, 19, was 5-foot-4 and seven months pregnant with her first child when a domestic squabble with her husband of one year turned deadly. The couple had a tumultuous marriage by any measure. Amber said her husband, Josh, a 6-foot-4, 225-pound former military man, had been abusive during their time together. During their short marriage, each had filed a restraining order against the other, but neither followed through. Amber and Josh had a history of domestic violence claims, and each spouse's family accused the other spouse of violence. His father said Josh wanted a divorce.[81] Her mother said Josh was an abuser.

The couple had only recently moved into apartment 2509 in University Club Towers, a 377-foot luxury high-rise known for its iconic circular structure overlooking Tulsa's scenic Riverside Drive. The posh apartment was a vacant second residence owned by Amber's parents, who offered it as a temporary residence to the young couple after their return from Josh's military duty in Alaska. The large plate glass windows on the 25th floor offered a breathtaking view of the tree-lined walking trails along the Arkansas River near downtown Tulsa.

It was late on a hot summer afternoon in June 2011 when a heated argument between the two turned into a shoving match. According to Amber, Josh, a military-trained Air Force recruit, grabbed her by the shoulders.

"He reached out and grabbed me. And I was pregnant. And he didn't care," she said. "So, I pushed him off me." Josh stumbled backwards into the corner of the living room, losing his balance and sending the full weight of his body crashing through the large plate-glass window behind him.

He frantically grabbed for the narrow window frame, looking at her in panic for one fleeting moment. Amber lunged for the window and tried to catch him by his foot as he fell, the shards of glass piercing her wrists. She couldn't hold on. His tennis shoe came off in her hand. She watched horrified as he fell, twisting and turning in the air, screaming as he descended, his arms flailing as he hurtled in a free fall onto the roof of the eight-story parking garage 17 stories below.

"It all happened in a split second," she said. "It was like the glass was not even there."

"Josh!" she screamed and ran to the elevator.

Alarmed tenants boarded the elevator to see the hysterical 19-year-old, her clothes bloodied from the shards of glass. Alerted by the commotion, the building manager boarded the elevator and yelled at her to shut up, not fully understanding what had just happened. She bolted out of the elevator on the first floor, then realizing her mistake, took the elevator back up to the roof of the parking garage, hoping Josh was somehow still alive.

What she found was forever burned in her mind.

"His bones were sticking out all over his body. His whole body was broken," she said. She rolled him over in her lap and tried frantically to push his body back into the shape it was supposed to be. Other residents peered over their balconies at the scene below, wondering what happened. A flurry of calls went out to 911.

Tulsa first responders rushed to the scene. A firefighter arrived at the top of the University Club Tower parking garage and found the body of Josh sprawled on the concrete and Amber leaning over him, sobbing, "I didn't mean to do it. I didn't mean to push him out the window."

Police/Fire Chaplain Rev. Danny Stockstill was going about his business that day when his pager went off. "Hey, you're up. We've got someone whose been thrown off a building downtown." Tulsa had 13 city chaplains, and it was Stockstill's day in rotation. He rolled up to the scene at University Club Towers and made his way to the roof of the parking garage.

"It's not my job to determine who's at fault," he said. "It's not my job to judge. I'm not the jury for anybody. I'm just trying to collect evidence so I can go make notification to the family."

He documented Josh's condition and checked on the wellbeing of firefighters, police, and paramedics. On his way out, he passed Amber's mom, Rhonda, and told her he didn't have a lot of answers yet and gave her his information. He and another officer then took off to find Josh's family.

"We walked up to the Hilberling' s door. Josh's mom opened the door and I told her who I was."

The first words out of her mouth were, "She killed him, didn't she."

An hour later, Amber was arrested and handcuffed as the prime suspect in the alleged murder of her husband. Amber's grandmother, Gloria, met her at the police station. She was led to a small room where they were left together after Amber's questioning by detectives. Amber was a wreck. The emotionally ravaged 19-year-old tried to make sense of what happened. She sobbed, cried, dropped her head to the table.

"Why did this happen?" she said. "This is stuff that only happens in movies." She buried her face in her arms on the table. "I killed him," she whispered.

"You didn't kill him, Amber," her grandmother said softly.

She said, "I'm only 19. I have the next 60 years to think about this, to let it torture me."

After her grandmother left the room, Amber could be heard talking to herself. "I will spend the rest of my life paying for this."

A police camera mounted in the room captured video of her conversation with her grandmother and herself alone. It would prove to be damning evidence at trial.

Judge Kurt Glassco presided over the trial, an imposing figure whose stature and reputation were both large and imposing. In addition to his role as a Tulsa Criminal Court Judge, he also served as a longtime pastor in a local Methodist Church

Assistant DA Michelle Kelley was assigned to prosecute the case. She was an aggressive legal prosecutor and pulled no punches in the courtroom when it came to crafting a first-degree murder case against Amber. She called Antonio DePaz, a window repairman, to the stand. He had been in the parking lot getting supplies from his truck when he said he saw a body fall out of the window. DePaz described Josh as falling "face-first" from the window, which Kelley said contradicted Amber's story that her husband stumbled backwards into the window. There were questions about how much DePaz could really see from 25 stories below, but his testimony became the linchpin of Kelley's efforts to cast doubt on Amber's innocence.

At the trial, Kelley's description of the couple's struggle morphed into the assertion that Josh went out the widow face-first, implying that Amber, pregnant and a foot smaller than Josh, had somehow heaved the 225-pound, toned and fit military man off the floor and hurled him out the window head-first.

In a prison interview in February, 2016, Amber told talk show host Dr. Phil that it was self-defense brought on by Josh's usual abusive behavior. Asked what the argument was about, Amber said Josh had plans to start selling pills again. Things turned physical when she accused Josh of being a coward. "The window wasn't supposed to happen." she said.

Amber's attorney, Jason Corn, agreed. The window should never have happened. After retrieving a piece of glass from the window frame in apartment 2509, he was astonished. It felt barely thicker than a napkin. The building's own window repairman testified that high-rise buildings normally use safety glass that is at least an inch thick, or more than ten times thicker than the thin sheets of glass of the University Club Tower windows. Once broken, he said, the brittle glass would disintegrate instantaneously into hundreds of small shards.

The low positioning of the window on the wall posed another risk. The windowsill was only 26" from the floor—dangerously close to the floor for a high-rise living room, especially when coupled with the building's choice of extremely thin glass.[82] An expert consultant hired by Corn said the circular building created air currents on that hot windy day that had the effect of sucking Josh out the window.

Amber's mother and stepfather were convinced Josh had abused Amber while in Alaska. They said he was using and dealing Oxycontin, a prescription opioid that delivers a powerful and fast high, known to be better than heroin. Corn claimed to have records from Eielson Air Force Base in Alaska revealing that Josh had been discharged from the military after only six months for misconduct that reportedly involved drug abuse.[83]

"He started doing drugs and wanting to sell them again and I was sad and disappointed and angry. That caused the fighting and everything that happened that shouldn't have happened," Amber told Dr. Phil.

During Amber's trial, a point of contention arose as to whether gruesome photos taken of Josh's body at the scene would be shown to the jury, photos showing Josh's skin burst open, bloody limbs lifelessly bent in unnatural directions, with exposed tissue and bone.

Assistant DA Kelley argued vigorously that the photographs were essential to prove that Josh fell through the window face-first, but her motive was clear: Studies show that gruesome photographic evidence evokes an emotional response from jurors that tends to adversely affect their attitudes toward defendants. Judges are cautioned to weigh the effect of "unfair prejudice" when admitting graphic evidence. After waffling on one particular photo showing Josh's face, eyes fixed and wide open, Judge Glassco yielded to Kelley's request.

Her ploy worked. The slideshow of 19 projected photos became a spectacle in the courtroom. Jurors were repulsed. In a matter of minutes, Amber became a villain. The DA's office offered Amber a no-contest plea with five years in prison and 15 years on probation, but she declined, convinced that a jury would find her innocent based on the facts.

She was wrong.

After two years of contentious legal proceedings, in March, 2013, a jury found her guilty of second-degree murder, and she was sentenced to 25 years in prison which, as Assistant DA Kelley noted, corresponded to the 25th floor from which Josh was pushed.[84] A second attorney for Amber appealed the case, but the appeal was denied. Under Oklahoma's current "85 percent rule," which was also applied to Miashah's sentence, Amber would serve at least 85 percent of her sentence before becoming eligible for parole.

Amber's long brown hair and good looks, coupled with the perception that she came from a life of privilege, made her a prime target for inmates at Mabel Bassett, most of whom had been exposed to the harsher side of life.

Amber, on the other hand, had never been exposed to the side of life she would encounter at Mabel Bassett with fist fights, threats, and extortion. On at least one occasion, she was reportedly badly beaten by another inmate.[85] According to inmates, meth was the medium of choice. You could get it—or get anything with it—depending on what you were willing to do or give up. The constant flow of drugs through the prison offered a constant temptation, a brief escape from reality, that most inmates craved. "Sometimes the guards look the other way," Amber said. "And other times they make deals themselves with the inmates, exchanging leniency and contraband for sexual favors." Shaking her head in disbelief, Amber said one girl had recently had sex with a guard in exchange for a small make-up mirror.[86] Any inmate who had been there for a while knew the ropes.

One of those who knew the ropes was a clean-cut 22-year-old Amber had befriended while both were awaiting trial in the Tulsa County jail. Her name was Jessica Parr.

"Amber was pretty much my friend from the git-go," Jessica said. "We kicked it. Like we had been friends before. We were tight. We got tight in Tulsa County [Jail]." Over time they became more than friends.

33

Buried above ground

JESSICA never had a chance to grow up normal.

"I don't know a life without meth," she said. "My mom started giving me meth when I was very young, like 13. She was on meth."

Jessica had an angelic face with smooth, flawless skin and a boyish blond cut scooped up in a rooster tail. She'd grown up in Italy where her father was a Navy officer. He had great hopes for his daughter. But she never stood a chance.

By 22, she was serving time in a minimum-security prison. At 27, she was on her second round at Mabel Bassett, serving a 17-year sentence for manufacturing meth and attempting to pawn stolen property. She was an unassuming, outspoken young woman whose fatal flaw was an unmitigated meth addiction inherited from her mother.

One of the girls she met in prison was Miashah. "When I met Moe, she was my first woman's bunkie at one point," she said. "She's a good woman. She's funny, she's always laughing. Prison caused me to be very skeptical of people and leery of people, and I put a wall up at first with Moe. But my first impression of her was real wrong. She gave me cigarettes and kitchen food, because we don't have any food. And that's wrong, but if you don't have anyone supporting you—or family members—the state pay you earn will barely buy your hygiene."

Being gay added a unique dimension to Jessica's prison experience. A number of other inmates were gay. Those who weren't sometimes yielded to their fellow inmates' sexual proclivities in order to placate their own desires in the absence of male companions. Inmates call it "going gay for the state," she said.

"Amber came to Mabel Bassett in May, 2013. I got there in July—and she became my girlfriend in October," Jessica said. Over time, Jessica came to know Amber's story well—the one she told the public, and the one she confided to Jessica.

"Josh never put a hand on her that day," she said. "Amber said she just made that up… If you think for one second that Josh was just beating on Amber, that's not the case. He was probably defending himself, because she was violent. She wasn't a broken-down single mother—it wasn't like that. I was with Amber for a year. She was a brat." Amber had a dark side, she said. "She beat up another girlfriend the first year-and-a-half of their relationship. She would hit her with a flat iron, punch her, slap her. Amber had a cold load slap. And she would take off on you."

It wasn't that Amber was naturally hostile; she wasn't born that way. According to Jessica, no one understood Amber, understood what she'd gone through as a child. "She was fucked up from an early age," she said. "Her mother fucked her up. She was a bridezilla in every way… constantly nit-picking, gotta look this way, gotta do this or do that." Amber could never do enough. She grew up an angry child. Drugs were her retreat.

"I think she and Josh were both on drugs, even though she was pregnant—opioids. And I think he was just sick of it. He was going to leave her. From her point of view, it was that *she* was leaving him. But I think he wanted to cut his losses. And he ended up dying… they were dangerous to each other." In Jessica's opinion, what it all boiled down to was that Amber never forgave herself for killing Josh. "But Amber didn't kill Josh," Jessica said. "Faulty windows and gravity killed Josh."

After her first ten years in prison, Jessica spent five years on the outside. She had no illusions about what landed her there a second time. "Meth has been all my problems. When I got out, I started manufacturing meth. And I got caught," she said. "But if you have a meth problem, the solution isn't to throw you in with all the meth." Which is exactly what she felt Mabel Basset had become—a haven for meth addicts. "There is no question where inmates get meth," she said. "You get it in the yard. Drug mules tossed packages over the fence. Inmates dealt it in the yard. Guards looked the other way. In the maintenance area, they had to put a third fence up to keep the packages from coming over. It's crazy." But still the drugs flowed in.

She was thrown into the "SHU," solitary confinement, more than once for 45 days at a time without daylight—a jail inside a jail. Walls within walls. "You go in there and the guards don't care about you a lot. The guards there assault you—I had my arm jerked up. They take your stuff when they search you, rip it up, throw it all together, throw your food in with your laundry soap."

During her second incarceration, something changed. "I met the Lord at Mabel Bassett, in the chapel there," she said. It was during an HIV scare. There was an orderly inmate that worked in medical who sold needles in the yard, and everybody was shooting up. And there was a rumor of HIV being spread around. "I almost lost my mind," Jessica said. "I was on meth, and I thought I'd contracted HIV. But through God's grace, I didn't." She was tested. She was clean. "That's when I knew the Lord was real. I wanted a better life. I haven't been doing meth since August 18, 2015, I stopped before I left Mabel Bassett."

By now, she knew the ropes. "At Mabel Bassett, the inmates kind of run things. You could pay your way to get whoever you want in your room. You pay the orderly. You just throw them some money." She started seeking out roommates who were clean. She didn't want meth in her room. It wasn't hard. The guards were lazy and they could be bought, she said. You just get cool with the guards or get cool with the unit staff. At Mabel Bassett, you can pay the guards to leave you alone."

Her voice trailed off, as if she were trying to resolve an unknown demon. "There's something in that prison, it's hard to explain. It's real bad. I have PTSD from Mabel Bassett." She'd seen people get stabbed, beaten up, and robbed by other inmates, and guards treated them like beings less than human. "They only make like $15 an hour," she said of the guards. "They're irresponsible, not professional. If you call your case manager on a guard, the guards will remember it. They're vindictive. At the end of the day, I've learned to mind my business."

Looking back, she feels like it took the time she got to 'get it.' If she'd only gotten a little bit of time, she'd still be in and out. "In

Oklahoma, they do you bad," she said. "There's a lot of women in Mabel Bassett that don't deserve the time they got. Their husbands abuse the kids, and the women go to prison for it.

*

34

The dead and the living dead

IT was nearly midnight on October 24, 2016, when Amber's mother, Rhonda Whitlock, received a voice message from the prison from an unknown person who said they needed for her to call back.

Her mother repeatedly called back but got no answer. "And so I kept trying, and then finally someone answered the phone," Rhonda said. "And I still don't know who it was, and they uttered three words: 'She is dead.' Click."[87]

Amber's roommate, Betty Hubbard, found her hanging from her bunk bed by the cord on her flat iron. Staff attempted to revive her, but after 15 minutes, she was pronounced dead. An official autopsy report confirmed she died from asphyxia due to hanging. She also had meth in her blood. Prison medics also found cuts on her wrists and forearms—signs this may not have been her first suicide try—but Amber's mother was adamant she was murdered. "I don't know if it finally just got to her and she snapped or if someone killed her," she told Dr. Phil in a November, 2016, follow-up interview.

Either way, she accused the correctional center of exposing her to conditions that "substantially increased the risk of harm to her."[88]

Only those on the inside could tell you what really happened, those who had known her for the duration of her incarceration and shared their innermost secrets—someone like Jessica Parr. "Something was wrong with her," Jessica said. "She was more than fractured. She never got over Josh. She didn't mean to kill him. She loved him and never forgave herself for that. It was such an oxymoron to be so independent and strong, and so broken. But something was wrong with Amber before that. She was suicidal as a teenager, she told me. She had a dark side when she was 16 or 17. Like she was trying to find something in herself."

Before Amber died, her mother filed a lawsuit against University Club Towers over the window. According to Jessica, she wanted Amber to sign full custody of Levi over so she could get more money. And Amber wouldn't do that; she didn't want to lose her son. "I think it was a combination of things that killed Amber," said Jessica. "Her mom stopped bringing Levi, stopped putting money on her books. Her mom uses her power. It's all about appearances, about money.

"And there was another factor. Amber was doing meth when it happened—and meth will intensify your demons. And lastly, she didn't want Levi's opinion of her to be tarnished. He was starting to get older and ask questions and stuff. And I feel like she just wanted to preserve his love for her, you know. But in the end, Amber killed Amber. And Amber killed Amber because she never got over Josh."

Amber's parents have Levi now, Jessica said. "I have pictures of him—and that is Josh's son. That is. That is his baby."

During the trials leading up to her incarceration, Amber had grown close to her attorney, Jason Corn. Shortly before her death, she sent him a letter. Included with the letter was a poem, a precursor of sorts for what lay ahead. It began:

So finally, I jump into the abyss of the unknown
silently as was my strength for so long…

It ended in a quiet resolve:

Opposing Life's own selfish claim to me,
Now I embody the simple quiet that I need.
Waiting on God from here…
I am okay.[89]

Amber was 25.

*

It wasn't expected. But it wasn't totally unexpected either.

"It really messed me up," Jessica said, "cause I loved her, you know."

With the end of Amber's life, a part of Jessica's prison life ended, too. She was transferred to a minimum-security prison in Oklahoma City, the final step for cycling out of the prison system. "When I get out, I want to have a relationship with my dad," she said, relaxing at the thought. "He writes to me but had a stroke last summer. He lives in New York. I haven't seen him in 12 years. Nobody has come to see me," she said, as if talking to herself. "But that's part of the learning experience."

With only a few months left until her July, 2017, release date, she doesn't know where she'll go next. But there's one thing she does know: Wherever it is, she's going to live it better this time.

"I just want to serve God."

35

Slaughterhouse 309

SOME stories of women trapped in the criminal justice system are like scenes ripped from the pages of a crime novel. One case in particular was especially grisly.

It was a hot afternoon in June, 2009, when Tammy was dragged across the floor of a cheap motel room to the shower. A white tank top was secured around her head with a belt to stop a tell-tale trail of blood on the floor. She had been pistol-whipped and beaten with a baseball bat for nearly an hour. Blood was all over the room. The brutal beating by her so-called boyfriend, Reginald, had started at a suburban house across town and continued in the backseat of his friend Joe's SUV. Reginald and his motel buddies were in a hurry to clean her up. The cops would be looking for them.

The cheap roadside motel served as a haven for addicts and drug dealers who needed rooms by the week. The dealers kept good track of one another. Everyone knew what room everyone else was in. Such was the life in the Route 66 Inn outside Oklahoma City. The rooms were small and dingy, and the walls reeked with the odor of cigarettes and noxious drugs. But in room 309, there was something else—the pungent smell of blood. By the time Reginald's rage was fully vented, Tammy, 26, had lost so much blood she was too weak to utter a sound.

Reginald, 34, was a beefy, 6-foot-tall black man known as "Candyman." He was an odd combination of good looks and the devil incarnate. He had taken Tammy under his wing a year earlier "to take care of her" when her haphazard life on the streets turned dangerous. But no one was more dangerous to Tammy than Reginald.

"Get her out of here," he told his buddies. It was 7:00 a.m. when they threw some sweats on her and hauled her to a clean room down the hall where a resident named Tasha was staying. He lifted up the mattress and shoved the half-conscious Tammy underneath between the wood casings where no one could see her. Lying on her back in the tomb-like enclosure, she could feel the blood running through her hair and pooling beneath her head.

Four hours later, she could hear the police going door to door on the outside walkway. They had already been to Reginald's room and had seen evidence of the bloody encounter. Within minutes they were pounding on Tasha's door: "*We're looking for Tammy McDermott. We know she's in there! We're not going anywhere until we find her!*"

Once inside, they looked everywhere—the shower, the kitchenette, the closet—there was no blood. "I could hear them talking, but I couldn't speak because I'd lost so much blood," Tammy said. "I couldn't talk. I couldn't scream."

It was then that an officer spotted drops of blood on Reginald's arm. That's all it took. An officer cuffed him and took him out. They knew Tammy was somewhere nearby. "*We're not leaving this motel until we find her, because there's blood everywhere down the hall—all over the balcony—and she may be dead somewhere.*"

By this time, Tasha was frightened and crying. “She’s under the bed,” she sobbed. They looked under the bed and couldn’t see her. They finally found her under the mattress wedged between the two side slats and carried her out on a stretcher.

“I’ll never forget the sound of them lifting me off the floor,” Tammy said. “Because my hair was stuck to my face and they were lifting me out of my own blood. And I couldn’t say my name.”

The gruesome scene in room 309 was the culmination of a cascade of horrific events that began earlier in the day—and a series of bad choices that got her there in the first place. It was the last time she ever saw Reginald.

*

Like Jessica, Tammy was raised on meth. A vibrant, striking 5-foot-5 brunette with enormous hazel eyes, she had spent the better part of her life trying to beat the odds. Outwardly invincible and full of wonder, she nonetheless had a proclivity for misadventure that inevitably led her down a rabbit hole.

Her mom was a user and her dad was a Vietnam vet, an alcoholic with PTSD. “He saw action in Vietnam. He’s in prison now,” Tammy said. “When he’d have flashbacks, they’d take him to the Northeast Oklahoma Correctional Center in Vinita, Oklahoma, for treatment.” But the state shut that down and started sending vets to the Jess Dunn men’s prison in Taft, Oklahoma. “So when my dad finally flipped out and tried to burn a house down with the ‘enemy’ in it, he was sentenced to five years at Jess Dunn.”

Tammy’s mom shared meth liberally with her daughter from Tammy’s young age through her teen years at Wagoner High. Her high school soccer coach had no reason to believe his champion varsity player was anything other than a bright-eyed, healthy young woman with a promising athletic future. She was offered a scholarship as a goalie at a European university and had every intention of attending. That is, until she discovered Xanax. Xanax, she said, joined meth as her new "best friend."

"You could go to doctors you heard about on the street and just tell them: 'This is what I want, this is for anxiety, this is what I've had before.' And they give it to you. I took it for anxiety."

But her anxiety never stopped.

When she was 18, things fell apart. She quit going to school, quit soccer, quit everything except drugs. She kept getting pulled over for drunk driving or for drugs. She was finally arrested for possession of meth and sent to the Wagoner County Jail for a month. It did nothing to deter her addiction. When she got out, she missed her "best friend" and needed money to buy drugs, so she got a job at a Dollar Store. After a short stay, she was charged with embezzlement. "It was nothin' big, but I needed it to buy drugs," she said. "When they caught me, I told the manager the truth and that I'd pay back everything that I'd taken, but she called the police and had me arrested anyway."

In 2005, she got her first taste of a truly rough life—*prison.* She was sentenced to eighteen months in Mabel Bassett Women's Correction Center. Her memory of that time was graphic.

"At Mabel Bassett, inmates demand that girls get on the phone and ask for money, because they didn't have money for cigarettes—threaten them, take them in the bathroom and beat them up... They just prey on those weak girls if they think they have money—give them attention. They look at them as new meat, like 'Hey, I'm gonna get that.' They make the girls even more weak and get their money." There were fist fights over drugs, she said. "They can take you to the bathroom where there are no cameras, or they take you to their cell, and if they have the right angle on the camera, guards can't see them."

*

When she went to the Wagoner County Courthouse in 2006 for her one-year review, they offered to release her with the provision that she complete a drug court program. It sounded good to Tammy—for all the wrong reasons. And as soon as she was released, she ran. "I ran to Oklahoma County. I was in desperation mode in Oklahoma City, not knowing anyone, always looking over my shoulder, coming close to death a few times. I'd just roam the streets, I'd strip, anything I could do to make it."

Three years later, she was nearly destitute and still roaming the streets. "I stayed mostly in motels until I found people who were cool, and I would stay in their house." That's when she met Reginald, a dope dealer. "He took me under his wing to make sure I was taken care of," she said. "But he would just tear me all the way down, every day. I ended up getting pregnant by him, and he hurt me. He was abusive to me." It was the beginning of the end in room 309.

She'd had his baby in that room.

It wasn't the life she wanted, and it wasn't the life she wanted for her baby. She needed to get out, but she didn't know how.

"I don't have a place to stay, I don't have a birth certificate, I don't have nothing." The next day she took the baby to the home of Jerry, a Vietnam vet who sheltered women. Jerry was already sheltering another girl, Melissa. Tammy hadn't been there long when Melissa took the baby and disappeared. Frantic, she called Joe, a friend of Reginald's, for a ride to find Melissa and her baby. Instead of coming to get her, Joe called Reginald. Tammy was waiting outside the house for Joe when she saw Reginald in the driver's seat of Joe's SUV pull straight up in the yard. "I could see the look on his face. He was mad. *I'd seen him like that before and knew the look*."

She ran in the house and locked the door, then headed to the back. Reginald jumped the back fence and came through the back door with a baseball bat before she could get out. He hit her with the bat and split her head open. Jerry got between them and tried to get him off, and Reginald hit him twice in the head with the bat. He then dragged Tammy out of the house by her hair and shoved her in the back seat of the car. Joe was driving. Reginald jumped in the passenger seat and continued to beat Tammy with the bat on the way to the motel. Midway, he pulled out a knife and cut off her hair. He then dragged her into the motel room and pistol-whipped her.

Jerry's neighbors saw the beatings from their yard and called 911. The police arrived within moments and took Jerry's statement, along with those of the neighbors who had seen the assault. Meanwhile, other drivers on the road saw the brutal backseat beating underway in the SUV and called police to report an assault in progress with a description of Joe's vehicle. An all-points bulletin was issued for the SUV, and police tracked it to down to the Route 66 motel. That's where they found Tammy half dead between the slats.

At the hospital, Tammy told the police everything—the baby, the beating, the drug dealings. The police went back to Jerry's house to retrieve Melissa's cell phone and began calling recently dialed numbers until they located Melissa and the baby. The Department of Human Services came and took the baby.

When she got out of the hospital five days later, the Oklahoma County District Attorney's Office sent her to jail for nearly $1,000 in old traffic tickets because Reginald was fighting his charges and the DA was taking him to court.

"They were just holding me there so I could testify against Reginald. And, of course, I didn't have a way to pay $1000. So I sat in there for seven months and then they pulled up another charge—like a possession charge—to keep me there."

Tammy was nervous. She knew that Reginald would kill her if she testified against him if he were ever released. "So I took everything back and told the DA I wasn't testifying because I was scared."

The Oklahoma County DA was hell-bent on prosecuting Reginald, but Tammy wasn't cooperating. "So he pulled up another charge—'intent to distribute'—even though they knew Reginald was the one dealing drugs, not me."

In the end, Jerry, the vet who had suffered Reginald's assault, and Tasha, who had witnessed the ordeal at the motel, gave written statements. Their statements, coupled with photos of Tammy's injuries, were enough to convict Reginald, and in October, 2010, he was sentenced to 35 years for kidnapping and assault and battery with a deadly weapon. After the trial, Tammy's charges were reduced from "intent to distribute" to "possession of a controlled substance," a felony in Oklahoma even though the substance in question was marijuana.

*

But this was not the end of her bad judgment. Out on her own again, her baby taken away and with few resources, she moved in with yet another man, Lorenzo, a 41-year-old tattooed Mexican man nicknamed "Cujo." Once again, she ended up pregnant. Lorenzo, it turned out, was a kingpin in a Mexican drug trafficking scheme and was wanted for murder. As with Reginald, when police tracked Lorenzo down, Tammy's mere presence in the house made her a co-conspirator in his operation, and she was charged along with Lorenzo and four others for drug trafficking and possession of proceeds.

Lorenzo, it turned out, had a grisly past with a history of violence. He was ultimately sentenced to life in prison without parole for first-degree murder. Tammy's charge was reduced from drug trafficking to "possession with intent to distribute," and she was sentenced to 20 years in prison. By now, she was almost nine months pregnant, so she was transported to the maternity ward on the top floor of the Oklahoma County Jail, a space she shared with a half-dozen other pregnant women.

"I knew I was about to go into labor. I had contractions that morning, so I just pushed the button and said, 'I'm going into labor.' And they always think you're lying—trying to get out of jail. It took them two hours," she said. Her contractions were four minutes apart when they finally called the doctor. She had the baby 45 minutes later *shackled to the bed.* But it turned out to be a blessing of sorts. "I got to stay with her for three days, breastfeed her, hold her skin-to-skin. Then I had to go back to prison. And that was the hardest thing ever. Just that rip-your-heart-out feeling." Her sister came and got the baby.

"But that right there saved my life, because I could get my head clear," she said. "If I'd kept on going, I would probably have ended up dead—or sold to the Mexicans. I really thought that was coming next."

She was transferred to the Eddie Warrior Correctional Center in Taft, Oklahoma, one of Oklahoma's minimum-security prisons designed to house women as they cycle out of the prison system. There, she saw the horrid state of women coming out of Mabel Bassett, where there isn't anything to do to pass the time except do drugs or get a girlfriend. "So many women come to Eddie Warrior from Mabel Bassett just looking sick because they're strung out on meth," she said. "Even if they go into Mabel Bassett half-clean, they come out strung out. They've been on drugs. They get it in the yard. You can put it like inside a ball and throw it over the fence. The guards give it to them for the right price. They don't pay those guards a lot so whenever they get money thrown at them, they take it."

According to Tammy, there were no drugs at Eddie Warrior, no way to get into that kind of trouble. If someone tried to smuggle drugs into Eddie Warrior, they were confiscated as soon as they hit the yard. "Someone is going to tell on them," she said. "That's not true of Mabel Bassett, where drugs are a part of life."

In the meantime, her baby was growing up without knowing her mother. The next time she saw her baby, she was three. "They had a play day at Eddie Warrior three times a year—and you get to play with them," she said. "I think she knew who I was without knowing me, because she would come up and lay her head on my chest." After that, Tammy's life began to change.

"Going to the chapel at Eddie Warrior was the intersection in my life… And I got to be a Christian and lost the desire for drugs… I was reading my Bible daily for over a year. They had an incredible chapel, and I completed the Victory Bible College program, a course where you take video classes on the whole Bible every day for nine months," she said. "It was an awesome experience, because I've never known the power of the relationship you lose. I totally changed my life in prison. I'm a totally different person. Every day I would pray, 'I'm ready, I'm ready.' And I just kept holding on and holding on."

In 2018, her sentence was reduced for good behavior, and a year later she was released with an ankle monitor—which she would wear 24-hours a day for a year on supervised probation. "It's like God opened up the gates of Heaven for me in my new life. Every step I'd take, everything just fell into place."

Sixteen years later, the baby taken from her during her ordeal with Reginald tracked her down from the small town where he lived in Oklahoma and met his mom for the first time. By now he was a strapping 6-foot-4 handsome kid with his mother's hazel eyes.

Even after their release into the community, women like Tammy live an extended nightmare. Many are left with real psychological trauma from a system that chews up their soul and spits them back out onto the street with little money and a fractured past that follows them for the rest of their lives.

It's worse if you're the wrong color and never had much of a chance to begin with. Families are shredded and children slip through the cracks of society, only to grow up and repeat the cycle they've been caught up in—more miscarriages of justice, more rushes to judgement, more handcuffs, more prison vans.

You can say these women should never have committed crimes in the first place. The truth is many of them never went to trial; they accepted pleas. Their only mistake was brushing too close to the fringes of Oklahoma law, which succeeds in doing what it does best—throwing women in cages.

"Once you get your name into the system, that's it. That first time. The cops in Oklahoma are going to be after you all the time," Tammy said.

"*This is the worst state ever.*"

*

PART 4

BLINDSIDED

The good, the bad, and the racist

36

Slammed by the system

MIASHAH had already spent over two years in the Tulsa County Jail, so transitioning to life inside Mabel Bassett prison walls was fairly painless. But one aspect was distinctly different: This time she would be staying for a very long time.

"I don't want to do anything to mess this up," Miashah said. She tried to avoid even the slightest jostle that might force her to relive the day of the fire. No parole hearings, no commutation. Nothing that would hurl her back into the spin cycle of Oklahoma's criminal justice system—and certainly not back into Judge Caputo's courtroom. There were many risks for a misstep. A guard could take a retributive dislike to her. An inadvertent mistake could add days to her sentence. She could be denied phone calls. Worse still, she could be sent to solitary confinement. Prison had become a drum beat she would march to. All she needed to do was keep marching until her sentence ran out. "I'm scared to death to make a move," she said. "The past is history to me now, you know."

But the past wasn't history for her mother. Chrisandria's future was permanently damaged. She could no longer muster the emotional stamina to drive a school bus of young vibrant children—a task that would only remind her of her grandchildren, Noni and Nylah. Meanwhile, her part-time nursing job in an adult care facility came to an ugly end when an aggressive news reporter, complete with a microphone and a camera man, showed up on the facility's front lawn. [90] The prospect of a reporter confronting her on live television about Miashah and her two dead granddaughters drove Chrisandria over the edge. She erupted at the reporter in a ballistic tirade. An elderly man on the porch in a wheelchair went berserk, and all hell broke loose in a shouting match. The manager interceded and Chrisandria was fired. "She knew my situation," Chrisandria said. "She knew what I'd been through, and she fired me anyway." She had been a nurse's assistant for 15 years. Her nursing career ended there.

Her life was on a steep downhill slide. She was a psychological wreck. To understand Chrisandria's extreme psychological crisis, you need only retrace the events was trying so desperately to forget: *The day of the fire.*

Not only had her two precious granddaughters been taken from her, but her two daughters had been caught in the undertow. Keahmiee was hospitalized for trauma, and Miashah was arrested in the hospital parking lot as a reported "arson suspect" when she went to visit her, leaving Chrisandria to struggle with questions for which she had no answers. In an attempt to put the pieces back together, a few days after the fire she drove back to Apartment #716—the burnt-out shell of the horrific scene.

"Before they got a chance to clean it up, I went into the apartment. It was too early really for me to go in there, but I was just so overwhelmed. There was a giant beam that had fallen down with one end slanted in the hallway... And when I saw that beam, I immediately thought about Nylah. The Fire Department reported they found her in the closet. But when I went to get the report, I waited for about two hours, and a fireman came out because I was upset and I was crying. He said nothing about the closet. He said Noni was under the bed in a blanket and that Nylah was in the hallway. He said a ceiling shaft fell in, and when they first went in, one of them stepped on the burnt shaft not realizing it was resting across Nylah's little body, that it snapped and crushed her head."

This gruesome depiction explained what she had seen at the hospital when she was asked by the coroner her to identify the children's bodies. Half of Nylah's face was gone. The horrific image of the chubby 18-month-old stoked her hatred and distrust of law enforcement and the entire judicial system.

To compound this crisis, Keontae had been arrested and slammed against a wall at the courthouse, Miashah was thrown in jail on trumped-up charges, and Keahmiee was arrested for "failure to appear" on a misdemeanor larceny charge she received three months before the fire. The larceny charge grew out of the pathetic state Keahmiee found herself in shortly before moving to London Square, one of the reasons she and Miashah had moved there in the first place. She had no money and nowhere to go and was sleeping with her kids at a vacant house owned by her grandmother Earleen. With two small children and little money to care for them, the young mother was running out of options.

Nylah, still a baby, needed milk. With no other means to feed her, she made her way to the baby food section at Walmart and took a can of baby milk off the shelf. A salesclerk saw her and notified the security guard, who called the police. The officer on call took one look at Keahmiee, a petite black girl lugging Nylah on her hip and little Noni clinging to her side and paid for the baby milk himself. Regardless, Keahmiee was charged with larceny from a retailer. With no reliable means of transportation to appear in court for the scheduled hearing on the charge and no money to pay the fine, a warrant for "failure to appear" was issued for her arrest, which laid in police files for nine months.

That is, until the police were called to a disruption at a southside apartment complex where Keahmiee moved after the fire at London Square. Although not involved in the disturbance, she was outside in the group when names were taken, and a routine warrant check brought up her outstanding "failure to appear" warrant. Still reeling from the London Square catastrophe only three months earlier—and the children for whom she stole the milk now stone-cold dead—she was arrested and handcuffed "in public view" according to the police report. She was then taken to the Tulsa County Jail for finger printing and a mug shot.

Adding to the emotional train wreck, a flagrant error about Miashah was uncovered on the Oklahoma Department of Corrections (ODOC) website. Although her conviction was clearly recorded by both Judge Caputo and DA Kunzweiler as *Child Neglect*, the public DOC offender website inexplicably showed *Child Abuse* next to Miashah's intake photo. Dennis Wharton, the bondsman who posted Miashah's original bond, was taken aback, and in May, 2019, he wrote a letter to Max Elliott, the ODOC Director, stating:

> "Inmates are likely to view Abuse of a child much more harshly than Neglect and seek to physically

> and mentally do her harm. In addition, it may well be that if Miashah was to appear before a parole board, some members, not realizing her offense was Neglect, not Abuse, could view her more harshly. Your correction to the DOC web site re this issue will be appreciated."

Elliott responded that the website error was a "computer glitch" that was "scheduled for correction." He said the error applied to all inmates sentenced for Child Neglect. How long the glaring error had been there or how long it would continue to appear was unknown. Regardless, Elliott displayed no sense of urgency and seemed oblivious to the damning consequence such errors could inflict on an inmate. As an example, a volunteer with a prison ministry group at Mabel Bassett reported that Rebecca, a fairly docile inmate, was, over a five-year period, literally beaten blind by other inmates who didn't take kindly to the charges posted against her. "I saw her several years earlier and she was fine," the volunteer said. According to Rebecca, prison medics performed surgery to restore her vision, which largely failed. She was told that further corrective surgery could not be performed due to lack of funds, leaving Rebecca still legally blind.

Chrisandria, for her part, was beside herself over the appalling website error in Miashah's charges. "*I don't know what they get out of this. It's pure evil. Because this is something that is never going away for the rest of her life. It ain't ever going away.*"

By this time, Chrisandria was more than fed up with the treatment of her family—and all people of color—in a state that had yet to shake the notion that all blacks were suspect. "Keahmiee didn't get arrested until after the babies died," she said. "You know, *their* people [white people] can do whatever they want to do and it's no big deal. But let a black person do something, with minor charges, you would think they'd murdered somebody. People don't know what it's like. I'm not saying *all* people don't know. *My people know.*"

With the possibility of her life in Oklahoma never returning to normal, she and Courtney made the decision to leave the state. It had been nearly a year since Miashah was sent to Mabel Bassett. "I can't put it back together here," Chrisandria said. "I've beat everything to death in Tulsa. I can't really grieve and focus here."

She and Courtney had family in Phoenix, Arizona, so in late 2016, they boarded a bus for Phoenix. The plan was to get their lives back together.

But as things turned out, their lives would never be put together.

37

Grief times two

AWAY from the daily reminders of the wreckage they left behind, the new environment in Phoenix afforded Chrisandria and Courtney a modicum of peace. Chrisandria landed a job with First Transit as a city bus driver, and Courtney was scheduled to start the next day at the city bus station gassing up busses. The two had been together 21 years, and for Courtney, it was love at first sight when the tall, attractive woman pulled up in a car next to him at a bus stop in Tulsa. Chrisandria and a friend were on their way to a store.

"Hey, you're riding a bus. Do you want to buy a car?" she asked.

"Yeah, I need a car," he said, so they exchanged telephone numbers. But before he could follow up, Chrisandria left town for six months. When she returned, she had a dozen voice messages on her answering machine. By this time she had forgotten who he was, so she deleted them. But Courtney hadn't forgotten her. He had gotten a close look at the tall, attractive young woman with distinctive scars across her chest, visible traces of her ex-husband's screwdriver attack.

Several weeks later, she and her sister were at a grocery store after church. "We were shopping, and this guy was following me all over the store. As I'm checking out, he runs up to the checker and starts bagging our groceries and asked, 'Ma'am, would you like some helping carrying these out?' When I opened the car door, I guess my coat fell open and he saw the scars on my chest. And he remembered them from the bus stop."

"It's you! You tried to sell me your car and I called and left messages," Courtney blurted out. Chrisandria wasn't really interested at the time but agreed to go out with him. That was August, 1996. They were married October 3, 1997 and had hardly spent a day apart since.

Still in love after 21 years, they found an apartment and had just begun to settle into life in Phoenix when Courtney received a disturbing call from Chrisandria's sister, Charlotte. He immediately tracked Chrisandria down at the transit station as she was boarding a bus for her daily route.

"I've got some bad news," he said.

She knew by his tone it was more than just bad news.

"Wait a minute," she thought. "I need to get ready for this." Her mind flipped through the possibilities. Her first thought was of her sister Lisa in Tulsa who had cancer, but she knew it wasn't that bad. Her next thought was worse: "Please tell me it's not one of my kids."

"No," he said. "Rico was killed in jail."

Rico was Charlotte's second son. He was an amicable but misguided young man who kept falling by the wayside and finally ended up in the Davis Correctional Center, a private prison in Holdenville, Oklahoma, a facility that housed inmates with addictions and those with special needs, along with the usual inmate population. He was sent to prison after an altercation in his home left Charlotte severely wounded and Rico's father dead from a gunshot to the head. Rico was sentenced to 38 years for second-degree murder and sent to Davis.

"He was just a normal kid until the month this actually happened," Chrisandria said. She had visited with Charlotte several times in the weeks leading up to Rico's attack. His doctors had diagnosed Rico with severe ADHD two years earlier and placed him on five or six medications. But when he turned 18, he was no longer covered by insurance, so they dropped him cold turkey, Chrisandria said. The medication came with a hefty price tag that his family couldn't afford. That's when Rico's bizarre behavior began.

His outbursts grew more erratic. Charlotte called Chrisandria and said Rico was acting crazy and had pulled a machete on his dad. A week later, she called back and said Rico had shot and killed his father and had wounded her in the process. Charlotte was taken to the hospital and Rico was sent to Davis Correctional Center.

The Davis Correctional Facility wasn't a place prone to fostering positive relationships. It offered troubled, angry souls like Rico a choice: to rehabilitate or die. Unfortunately, Rico was one of those who died.

In July, 2017, a prison guard found him dead in his prison cell during a routine cell check prior to sending inmates to the showers. The circumstances of his death were unclear and delivered by prison officials in vague bits and pieces. When prison officials first notified Charlotte of Rico's death, they said he died of "natural causes."

"Bullshit!" Charlotte said. "That's Bullshit! Rico was only 28 years old!" They hung up, saying they would look into it. They called back the next day with a different answer: Rico had been strangled and beaten to death by his cellmate. When Charlotte drove there to identify his body and pick up the pictures, she told Chrisandria that Rico was beaten so bad that you couldn't even imagine how somebody could mix that up with natural causes. "Teeth knocked out, neck obviously broken, beat completely up, blood under his fingernails—cause you could tell he was fightin.'"

Rico's body was found on the bottom bunk of his cell where his cellmate dragged him after a brutal attack over what he described as a personal issue. During the autopsy, the medical examiner found two tattoos on his body: a tattoo that read "ONE!" on his left forearm, and a tattoo of praying hands on his right, seemingly the signs of a young man intent on turning his life around.

When Rico entered the prison, Charlotte was told he would be kept in a maximum-security unit away from the general prison population. But eventually he was housed with another troubled inmate, a move that turned fatal.

Davis Correctional Center was one of three private prisons operated by CoreCivic, a for-profit prison operation contracted by Oklahoma to house the state's growing prison population. Rico's death was one of a string of homicides at the facility in a 10-month period. Two inmates were strangled to death and one was stabbed to death by other inmates. The mounting number of inmate homicides brought a slew of lawsuits against the facility, including one from Charlotte. The state of Oklahoma paid CoreCivic nearly $30 million a year to manage the Davis Correctional facility with the expectation that inmates would be housed—not killed.[91]

Miashah was going about her normal prison routine at Mabel Bassett when the news came of Rico's death. She and Rico had been close. They were born only a week apart and grew up celebrating birthdays together.

"He was different than most urban kids," she said. "That's just the way it was. And they shunned him. And when he finally had a total breakdown, I mean, where do you go for help? He didn't have a support system. And when he was going through that, his mom did the best she could, but he was shunned."

Now in prison herself, Miashah could only imagine the troubles of someone with psychological issues like Rico. "I never understood when I was on the outside how real messy prison is. It's dangerous in here—I don't care if you're male or female—it's prison. But it's especially dangerous in a men's prison—real dangerous."

*

Rico's funeral was the following week. The thought of returning to Oklahoma was abhorrent to Chrisandria. She and Courtney had been in Phoenix for only two months. But a member of the Moses family never missed a family funeral, so she called her superintendent and requested a substitute driver. She and Courtney were scheduled to board a bus for Tulsa the next morning to attend Rico's funeral.

Courtney hadn't been feeling well the night before, so Chrisandria decided to let him sleep. "We were talkin', and all of the sudden he said, 'I'm tired, sweetheart, and I love you, but I'm going to bed.'" He walked to the bedroom and laid down. Chrisandria could see him from the kitchen. The way he laid down was odd, but she didn't think anything of it.

"It was kind of like he fell down on the bed. And I'm thinking, 'Ok, he's just tired.' I got done cleaning up the kitchen and walked into the bedroom and said, 'Scoot over, I need to get into bed.' And he stuck his arm straight out, you know, and then it just dropped.

And I still didn't… my mind just wouldn't let me think anything was wrong. And I laid down and slept all night."

*

At daybreak, Courtney wasn't up yet, so Chrisandria decided to walk to the grocery store for coffee and rolls and wake him up when breakfast was ready.

"It was so strange," she said, looking back. "I don't remember walking to the store. I don't remember going into the store. I don't remember getting the food. I just know that when I got in the house, I put the muffins in the oven and he wasn't up. And I started yelling at him and fussing like I do. And I turned around and he wasn't snoring. I knew instantly something was wrong. I can't explain it, but I knew instantly."

Courtney had been placed on several medications by different doctors: pethidine with oxycodone and gabapentin. He had COPD, diabetes, and severe asthma. "And he had started to breathe funny. His left arm was getting noticeably smaller. When he went to the doctor, they couldn't find anything wrong. And looking back, I should have known. I was so busy getting stuff together I couldn't really focus on it."

Without really comprehending the situation, she went to the sink and poured a glass of water. "And I was still kind of fussing. And I walked into the bedroom, and I thought, 'He's going to start trippin' when I dump this water on him.' And at the same time, I had this feeling. And I threw the water on him, and he didn't move. And I yanked him off the bed and onto the floor and started doing CPR. And when I did, I looked down. His lips were blue and his fist was clenched. I called 911 and everyone started coming over and trying to help.

"I knew he was gone, though. I knew he was gone."

At Mabel Bassett, Miashah stared at her unit manager in disbelief. A message had arrived from Keahmiee: *Courtney was dead.*

It had only been two weeks since Rico's death. And now Courtney was dead. Miashah was devastated. "He was my biggest cheering squad," she said. "It took me a while in life to understand about he and my mom and what he went through for us. When I was growing up, he was just 'Courtney,' because I never knew my dad. I was young and didn't have a standard for all that daddy stuff, but he did—and he just kept holdin' on. He had nerves like ice. And when I got older, *I understood he was a better dad than my real dad could have been.* He held my whole family together. It took a while for me to understand the sacrifices he made and all the things he went through for my mom's sake, 'cause I had a path of my own. And by the time I realized it, he was gone. The last letter I got from him was on my birthday. It arrived August 2, 2017, the day before he died." It read:

> Miashah, time is passing. Your mom and I are doing everything we can to make you happy. Be looking out the window because I'll be coming to see you someday. Love, Pops.

But Courtney would never be coming to see her.

*

38

The hungry jaws of the law

IN the weeks before moving to Phoenix, Chrisandria had received a check she said was reimbursement for a faulty outdoor pool the family had purchased sometime earlier. The check for $1,984 arrived in the mail and looked legitimate. She had no bank account, so took the check to a local northside check-cashing store where she was greeted by a heavy-set, gray-haired man behind a glass window. Courtney waited in the car.

"Is this real?" she asked, sliding the check under the window.

"Let me see your license," he said, and asked her to endorse the check. She did as she was asked and shoved the check and her driver's license back under the window. He took the items and headed for a back room to see if it was real, Chrisandria assumed. She took a seat in a metal chair at the front and waited.

The next thing she saw were police officers barging through the door next to her. The pawn shop owner had called the police and said the check was forged. After instructing her that she was under arrest, the cops rifled through her purse and found other evidence they considered incriminating. She was handcuffed, driven downtown, and booked for "uttering a forged instrument," a felony. The detective who interrogated her was rugged and rude, Chrisandria said. "She had mousy brown hair, and she was so angry."

"You were just going to take that money and run. You're going to jail," the officer announced.

"How were you going to charge me with uttering a forged instrument if I didn't even know it was forged?" Chrisandria exclaimed.

"That's how we set this up. The pawn shop calls us when someone comes in with a bogus check."

"That's entrapment!" Chrisandria shot back.

"She started talking to me about the check, and then it segued into Miashah. So now I'm getting irritated," Chrisandria said. "The way you talk is very disrespectful to my child, which has nothing to do with the check," she told the officer. She had little recourse to defend herself, although she knew it didn't matter anyway. She was booked for forgery. "A felony is now on my record and I can't get a job," she sighed. The check was indeed forged, and she had "uttered" it for cash. Courtney called a friend who bonded her out of jail.

By this time, she was nearly broke and now more distraught than ever. The fines and court costs would plunge her into debt for months to come, maybe years. Even if she did find a job, it wouldn't leave her enough money to make ends meet. She still had a younger child, Nubia, living at home.

"I had family in Tulsa, but nothing was working there," Chrisandria said. "I couldn't put it back together, you know." That's when she and Courtney set their sights on Phoenix, glad to be leaving it all behind.

As it turned out, it wasn't all left behind. They had no sooner left Oklahoma than remnants of the check fiasco began to unravel.

The Tulsa bondsman who posted her bail was livid. He was on the hook for her failure to appear on a $2,000 bond and determined to find her wherever she was. Although he publicly promoted himself as a communicator "with the ability to listen to people… have compassion for them, their needs and fears," he tracked Chrisandria down in Phoenix and dispatched a beefy black bail enforcer, armed with a bullet-proof vest, a badge, and a gun, to drive 1,065 miles from Tulsa to Phoenix to arrest her.

Courtney's ashes were barely cool in the urn when, just six months after they moved to Phoenix, the bail enforcer showed up at her apartment door, gun drawn, ordering her to put her hands behind her back. She was cuffed and driven back to the Tulsa County Jail for failing to appear on her charge of uttering a forged instrument with a willful intent to defraud.

Whether she or any of the hundreds of people who present a disputed check had the actual "willful intent to defraud" is questionable. Some law enforcement agencies decline to press charges when contacted by banks in this situation, viewing the individual who cashed the check as a victim in the scam.

But Chrisandria was black and she lived in Oklahoma.

*

There was no way she would be cleared to visit Miashah now, since anyone with a felony record was prohibited from visiting inmates in Oklahoma, relative or not.

"I can't send her any money 'cause I'm still paying fines," she lamented. "I make $300 a week! I can't even get a decent job. They won't let me drive a bus because I have a felony on my record. Tulsa

Transit let me go through the whole process and training and then they said something's popped up on my background. And I told them I had a background! I told them I had a felony. It's not drugs, it's not murder, it's not child abuse, none of that. *But I can't drive a bus because I have a felony?*"

Caught in the grip of depression, persecution, and overwhelming sorrow at the death of Courtney, her only true love, just waking up in the morning became a challenge. Then, her sister, Lisa, died of ovarian cancer the day after Courtney's funeral.

"I've had so much to deal with the last five years—losing Courtney. Rico died a couple of days before Courtney, and then losing my sister Lisa to cancer three weeks later. I feel like once Courtney left, everything fell down. I miss him. I don't see it ever being alright. I think about him constantly—like all day, every second."

"Give it some time. It'll fade," a friend said.

"I'm not sure I want it to," she sighed.

She gathered up the remnants of her broken life and faced the troubled road ahead.

"Just keep breathing," she told herself. "Keep breathing."

*

39

Same song, different color

CHRISANDRIA'S first clue that life in Oklahoma hadn't changed since she left came on October 20, 2017, when she opened the morning headlines: "Robert Bates released from prison after serving one-and-a-half years of a four-year sentence for killing Eric Harris."

It was difficult to keep up with the lies that had unraveled since the April 2, 2015, police shooting of Eric Harris that left him dead.

Bates, the now 76-year-old millionaire insurance executive who moonlighted for years as a reserve Tulsa County sheriff's deputy had been sentenced to four years in prison by a jury for manslaughter in the death of Eric Harris. The bumbling man had become a Tulsa sheriff's deputy volunteer based on bogus training paperwork and had shot Harris point blank in the chest when he mistakenly grabbed his Smith & Wesson instead of his taser. [92]

Bates was reportedly asleep in his SUV and appeared disoriented when aroused for an undercover illegal gun sales sting. Before long, Harris was being restrained face-down on the pavement by officer Michael Huckaby, who had his knee on his neck. Suddenly, a single gunshot rang out.

"Oh, I shot him," Bates said after pulling the trigger. "I'm sorry."

His weak apology didn't fly with Chrisandria. Bates, a white man, "was sorry" for shooting an incapacitated man and was released after serving only 18 months in prison. Chrisandria's daughter, Miashah, a black woman, was also sorry for the accidental deaths of her two nieces when she merely left to take out the trash, but she was sentenced to 15 years in prison.

Miashah was still behind bars when Bates walked out into the parking lot at the North Fork Correctional Facility in the predawn hours, wearing a jacket with the hood up. He was accompanied to a waiting SUV by what appeared to be security guards.

After the fatal shooting, it emerged that Bates had repeatedly bent the rules. A 2009 internal memo written by a sheriff's sergeant alleged that superiors knew Bates didn't have enough training hours and that the sergeant was pressured by others to look the other way because of Bates's close relationship with Sheriff Stanley Glanz.

Deputies had voiced concerns about Bates's behavior since he joined the reserve force. When confronted, Bates reportedly said that he could do what he wanted and that anyone who had a problem with that should talk to Sheriff Glanz.

Bates had worked for a year as a police officer between 1964 and 1965 and had returned as a reserve deputy in 2008. He chaired Tulsa County Sheriff Stanley Glanz's re-election committee in 2012 and purchased five vehicles for the Violent Crimes Task Force on which he served. Bates had also partially funded a previous joint trip with Glanz to the Bahamas, although Glanz said, "It didn't have any influence."[93]

In November 2014, Sheriff Glanz resigned over the shooting death of Eric Harris and was sentenced in 2016 to a year in jail, but his sentence was suspended by a judge after he pleaded no contest to willful violation of the law and failure to perform official duties.

In federal filings, other Tulsa County sheriff deputies claimed that Harris caused his own shooting death with his "unlawful and criminal conduct," stating Bates's actions were "objectively reasonable" and "in good faith." [94]

Bates was released from prison with nine months of DOC supervision. His early release included stipulations that he refrain from drinking alcohol and entering establishments where alcoholic beverages are served, not using or possessing drugs unless prescribed by a doctor, and not associating with anyone who has a criminal record. The latter rule was notable since his longtime friend Sheriff Stanley Glanz was convicted of two misdemeanors and therefore had a criminal record.

After his release, Bates appeared to flagrantly ignore these stipulations. He was spotted three months later drinking alcohol at an Oklahoma bar with his wife. When another patron spotted him, he recorded a short video clip and send it to the Harris family's attorney. The patron stayed long enough to see Bates consume several drinks of what looked like white wine, saying it "looked like he was kicking back a few." [95] Punishment for a parole violation is decided at the discretion of parole officers and can include a return to prison, house arrest, wearing a GPS monitor, more frequent urine analysis tests, and other measures. There was speculation as to whether a black person is more likely than a white to have probation or parole revoked for similar violations considering Tulsa's record of racial injustice.[96] There is no public record of punishment for Bates's probation violations.[97]

Eric Harris's brother, Andre, said Bates should have known that he was not supposed to be in a restaurant that serves liquor. "When any convicted felon gets out before the end of his sentence, he knows the deal: If you don't abide by the rules, then you risk going back to prison," Andre said.

Attorney Dan Smolen, whose law firm represented the Harris family in its lawsuit against Bates, put out a statement about the former reserve deputy serving less than half of his sentence. "He is being released in time to celebrate Thanksgiving and Christmas with his family. He is being released as Eric Harris's family continues to mourn his death," Smolen said. "Now that Mr. Bates is out of prison, it is our expectation that the civil suit filed against him and former-Sheriff Glanz will finally begin to intensify."

In March, 2018, it did just that. Smolen secured a $6 million settlement for excessive force in the Harris family's lawsuit against the Tulsa County Sheriff's Office. The civil suit alleged that Bates was neither properly trained nor supervised and accused former Sheriff Stanley Glanz of turning "a blind eye to these dangers" to allow his friend and financial benefactor to 'play cop' on the streets of Tulsa County.

"It's not just a race issue, it's a dehumanization issue," said Smolen. The law firm also reached a $1.7 million settlement with Michael Huckaby, the officer who kneeled on Harris's head as he was shot. Smolen noted that Huckaby's father, Thomas Huckaby, was a supervisor at the Tulsa County Jail when black employees filed a discrimination lawsuit against the department, and that he had signed off on some of Bates's timesheets. Up to this point, the Tulsa County Sheriff's Office had been spinning the truth and fending off questions on Bates's age, false training records, and his involvement in the Violent Crimes Task Force.

"This will be the first time that the world sees what an officer that vows to protect and serve actually does after a bad shooting," said Smolen. "When Eric Harris was shot, we came out publicly and said we're going to show you what happens when you try to cover up a bad shooting. We weren't just talking about that shooting, we were talking about how, for a decade, this was a corrupt—*and corrupt to the core*—Sheriff's Office."

Smolen said that the community now holds "genuine hope" there can be "some measure of justice and accountability" when law enforcement violates the rights and takes the life of a black citizen.

Smolen said, "From the darkness of tragedy came the light of public scrutiny and a seismic shift in perception and awareness in a city with a long history of racial division, injustice, and violence... Eric's death, and the profound government corruption uncovered in the wake of his death, serve as a wake-up call for Tulsa."[98]

Andre Harris remembers how Robert Bates's defense labeled his brother a dangerous criminal. During his trial, Bates's attorney, Guy Fortney, told jurors that Bates is "somebody we should be proud of" because he exited his SUV to "man up" and help capture a fleeing felon. "I don't have to call Bates a superhero; he's a convicted felon," Andre said, thanking God for the settlement that would allow Eric's son to pursue an education.[99]

The "wake-up call" Smolen referred to had not come easily. It had wrenched and twisted itself through long-standing prejudice and cronyism in the Oklahoma criminal courts into the light of day,[100] writhing its way through two judges of opposing views before landing in the lap of one who could maintain a solid grip on the case, Judge James Musseman.

Judge Caputo had originally been assigned to preside over Bates's preliminary hearing, and in spite of documents showing a potential conflict of interest, he declined to recuse himself, saying the oath he took as a judge was to follow the law "without bias, prejudice, or sympathy." Caputo had previously been a Tulsa County sheriff's deputy himself and had known Sheriff Stanley Glanz for more than 20 years. Caputo's daughter was also a civilian employee of the Tulsa County Sheriff's Office. Regardless, he refused to recuse himself.

That all changed six months later when it was revealed he had been legal counsel for one of the witnesses to the Harris shooting in two divorce proceedings. On the fifth floor of the Tulsa County Courthouse, prosecutors intervened and asked Judge Caputo to recuse himself. The black activist group Black Lives Matter was also raising public objections in light of Caputo's past prejudicial rulings. The mere perception of partiality did not bode well given the racial climate. Also, Caputo was up for re-election November 4, 2018, less than a month away. On October 29, he finally recused himself from the case.

The next judge in line for the case was Judge Sharon Holmes, Miashah's original pro bono attorney who resigned from Miashah's case in 2014 and who had now assumed the bench. Holmes also recused herself, noting that Smolen, the attorney representing Eric Harris, was listed as a campaign contributor for her election committee.

Judge Musseman accepted the case without controversy.

Although Caputo had cited his integrity "as his most important asset both on and off the bench," he himself was soon caught in the whipsaw of law enforcement for his own activities off the bench.

*

40

What goes around comes around

THE timing couldn't have been worse.

Judge Caputo, 59, had been a district judge for eight years, and his re-election bid was now only three weeks away. The judge was usually seated at the head of his courtroom in 506, but in late October, 2018, he found himself in the hot seat after allegations surfaced that he was a client of a massage business known for prostitution.

A suave-looking man of Italian descent, he was known for his staunch support of breast cancer research, where he donned a pink judicial robe to ride a pink-clad horse for breast cancer awareness, and for the mass marriage ceremonies he presided over at the courthouse for dozens of smitten brides in white wedding gowns smiling up at their happily-ever-afters. At a popular local bar, he was the guy with the open shirt and gold chain bracelet.

His penchant for wrestling surfaced in 2015 when he was named a guest referee for a pro wrestling bout at Tulsa's Expo Square Pavilion. The story was splashed across Tulsa papers with photos of Caputo ringside, his muscles bulging out of a striped referee shirt.

He was billed on the bout card as "Mr. Justice." His fascination with pro wrestling started as a youngster with the championship wrestler Bruno Sammartino, who was also Italian. He always wanted to be a wrestler, but said he was six inches too short and 50 pounds too light to compete. At the time of the massage parlor allegations, a Facebook video showed Caputo stripped to the waist, displaying six-pack abs that any buff 21-year-old would be proud of. The muscled magistrate worked out at a gym at 5 a.m. every day and once entered, and placed, in a Mr. Oklahoma bodybuilding contest.[101]

Judge James Caputo (Courtesy: The Lost Ogle)

As a long-standing judge, he easily defeated his election opponents, and what he lacked in size on the wrestling circuit he made up for with a commanding presence in the courtroom. Defendants quaked at his presence, and attorneys on both sides cow-towed to his judicial whims. Miashah witnessed Caputo's judicial knack for bending the law when he told her that she could withdraw her guilty plea within ten days—and then denied her attempt to do so. Dismissing her claim of possessing new evidence—evidence that was unknown to her when she entered her plea—he retracted his earlier statement that she could withdraw her guilty plea with the bifurcated statement that, regardless of the evidence, she had "knowingly" entered her plea, which sent her to prison for a third of her young life.

Miashah later learned from other inmates at Mabel Bassett with the misfortune to have been caught in his claws that this wasn't the first such ruling by Caputo. But it was to be one of his last.

Caputo was reportedly going about his daily routine in October, 2018, when an agent with the Oklahoma Attorney General's office appeared in his chambers and said the office had undisputed evidence, including audio, video, and texts, that Caputo paid for sex at a massage parlor. If he resigned, the agent said, it would end right there. If not, the Attorney General's office was going to take the matter to a grand jury and intended to prosecute him.

Two months earlier, police had shut down the Phase 2 Spa and the Phase 3 Spa in Tulsa after a human trafficking investigation led to several arrests. A witness at the parlor identified Caputo as a customer and claimed she had sex with the judge. Multiple employees reported the business was run "solely for the purpose of prostitution." One employee was identified as a 17-year-old girl.

Not one to be easily intimidated, Caputo refused to step down. News of the salacious allegations spread quickly to every corner of the local broadcast media. With his re-election now dangling precariously in the winds of public scrutiny, the campaign of his young female opponent, Tracy Priddy, a successful former prosecutor, was gaining ground.

Caputo's campaign had already drawn controversy after being reprimanded for using jurors' addresses to send them mailers asking for their vote. His confident swagger and somewhat egotistical demeanor, along with his history of controversial decisions, appeared to have placed him in the crosshairs of the powers that be.

During a public statement, Caputo sat before reporters with the dyspeptic demeanor of someone in need of an anti-acid, a river of sweat breaking out on his face. His predicament, if proven, was no less of a crime than many of those he had sent to prison. At the news conference, he asked for the presumption of innocence to apply to him as it should to anyone accused of criminal activity. However, if he was to be treated like he did Miashah Moses, he would receive very little leniency.

Narcotics agents were also involved in the judge's case. An undercover agent posing as a prostitute had met with the judge, law enforcement sources said. Caputo reportedly sent her a text message about having a "threesome." Caputo disputed the allegation. He claimed that he received an invitation to meet about three weeks earlier from a woman who reached out to him on Facebook and that he had never offered payment for sex.

"I am a single man," he said. "And the meeting was represented to be a social get-together at a local restaurant." He said the woman had been with another woman when he arrived but that the second woman had left a few minutes later.

"A few days later, I was asked to meet the other lady who was briefly at the restaurant. I agreed to meet her at a local restaurant," he said. "During the conversation, she announced she saw men for money." Caputo said he reserved appearing judgmental and soon after concluded the conversation and left.

His allies in the courthouse, otherwise viewed as towering symbols of justice, began to run for cover. DA Steve Kunzweiler quickly sent a letter to the Attorney General's Office asking that his office be recused from looking into Caputo. In the letter, Kunzweiler wrote that his office had a "working relationship" with "a person named as a patron of this establishment."[102]

Caputo dug his heels in. "I told the assistant attorney general and the young woman with him that I had never been to an illicit massage parlor in my life and that I had never engaged the services of a prostitute." Speaking at a public briefing with his attorney, Clark Brewster, at his side, Caputo declared, "I want to serve the people as their judge like I have the past eight years. I pray that this last-ditch, salacious, and false attack upon me will be seen for what it is. I believe that all life experiences bring lessons and self-reflection. This nightmare will heighten my sensitivities to false accusations during the balance of my judicial career."[103]

His personal revelation came too late. On November 6, 2018, Caputo lost his re-election bid to Tracy Priddy.

Judge Sharon Holmes, on the other hand, was re-elected to a second term in a landslide. Caputo's courtroom was now hers.

41

Eyes wide shut

JUDGE Caputo's bench was still warm when Judge Sharon Holmes assumed his seat in courtroom 506, and with it a fresh new perspective on justice.

From the moment she donned her judicial robe in 2014, Holmes was a formidable presence in the courtroom. As the first black female judge elected in Tulsa County, she launched into a raft of racially charged cases with the same judicial craft and vigor she had exercised as Miashah's pro bono defense attorney. She could slice and dice the truth from the best and worst arguments. She was unshakeable. An ex-military prosecutor and former Tulsa assistant district attorney, she could separate fact from fiction with the laser precision of a ninja.

The District 1 population she represented encompassed the infamous Greenwood district and much of north Tulsa's predominately low-income black community whose rights had been trampled for decades. Her district spanned both sides of the railroad tracks that divided north side black communities from their white victimizers on the south side during the brutal rampage of the 1921 Race Massacre.

The powerful judicial seat put Holmes in line to hear a variety of controversial cases that exposed the raw cultural biases still simmering between north side residents and the police officers assigned to protect them. She had no sooner assumed her seat on the bench when one such case landed on her criminal docket.

Honorable Judge Sharon Holmes (Courtesy: Tulsa World)

Jeremy Lake was 19 years old when he was murdered in cold blood by Shannon Kepler, an off-duty Tulsa police officer. It happened late one evening in August 2014.

"I really hope they rot in prison for a very long time," sobbed Lisa Kepler, 18, whose parents were accused of killing her boyfriend Jeremy right in front of her.[104] Her mother Gina Kepler was in the passenger seat when Lisa's father got out of his car and started shouting at Lisa. Shannon and Gina Kepler, both white, were 24-year veterans of the Tulsa Police Department. Lisa turned in her parents, saying her dad shot her boyfriend to death in the street and then fired at her as she ran. ·

Lisa's parents, who had adopted Lisa and her two sisters when she was eight-years-old, kicked her out of the house the week before and dropped her in front of the Tulsa Day Center for the Homeless with nothing but the clothes on her back. There, she met Jeremy, a mixed-race black youth, and they began dating. Jeremy often spent time during the day visiting the Day Center to check on the homeless people who camped in the surrounding area, taking them water, snacks, and blankets. Jeremy lived in a small house with his aunt and invited Lisa to stay with them.

After seeing a Facebook post by Lisa saying she had developed a relationship with Jeremy, officer Shannon Kepler, in violation of police policies, purportedly used police resources to pull the records of Jeremy Lake, including his home address. They then took Gina's black Chevy Suburban and confronted Jeremy in front of the house at about 8:45 p.m. Lisa and Jeremy were walking home from the center when the Kepler's SUV pulled up and her dad yelled, "What the hell are you doing here?" Lisa turned and walked away.

When Kepler exited the Suburban, Jeremy faced Shannon Kepler and attempted to introduce himself. Jeremy's brother Michael, 12, and Josh, a friend of Jeremy's, watched from the porch of Jeremy's aunt's house. In less than ten seconds, Shannon Kepler pulled his .45-caliber revolver and pointed it at Jeremy, who was standing unarmed ten feet away. He fired and hit Jeremy three times.

As Jeremy was being murdered by her father just twenty feet away, Lisa screamed in sheer terror and ran toward the house. She tried to hide behind a sparse lilac bush as her father fired twice more in her direction. The shots missed her but ricocheted off the house, injuring young Michael, who was still on the porch. Lisa called 911 and reported the shooting. Police arrived and found Jeremy's body in the street in front of his aunt's home.

Shannon Kepler, 54, was accused of first-degree murder and shooting with intent to kill. Gina Kepler, 48, was accused as an accessory to murder. Shannon told investigators Jeremy was armed and that he shot Jeremy in self-defense. Their cases were tried separately.

Race was not initially a point of contention, but it became a bigger issue as Shannon Kepler's attorney, Richard O'Carroll, sought to "systematically" strike black potential jurors from the final panel. O'Carroll and members of the Tulsa Police Department reportedly wanted "a white judge," but efforts to recuse Holmes were unsuccessful. In a final, tense exchange with O'Carroll, Holmes announced abruptly, "The proceedings are finished." She then rose from the bench and exited the courtroom.[105]

Shannon's first trial in 2015 ended in a hung jury.

He was granted a second trial in 2016, during which DA Steve Kunzweiler, who was supposedly prosecuting Kepler, delivered his closing argument with a jaw-dropping five-minute tribute to Shannon Kepler, praising his 24 years of service. One courtroom observer questioned the prosecutor's sincerity in finding justice for Jeremy, saying it "sounded like Kunzweiler, the prosecutor, was reading from the closing argument of the defense."[106] That jury also deadlocked.

In the third trial in mid-2017, Kepler's daughter, Lisa, testified about the night of the shooting, telling jurors that as they were walking to the house, she heard her father ask Jeremy what he was doing. She walked away and had her back turned when she heard gunshots.

"I turned around and saw Jeremy hit the ground," Lisa said. "I ran and hid behind the bush that was in the center of the yard."

During cross-examination she told Kepler's defense attorney that she could say "with certainty" that Jeremy didn't have a gun with him at the time.

After three years and three hung juries, in October 2017 a fourth jury found Shannon Kepler guilty. He was sentenced to 15 years in prison and led from the courtroom in shackles, looking tired and disheveled in a striped black jumpsuit. Charges against Gina Kepler were dropped due to lack of evidence that she participated in the crime.

Shannon, then 57, took early retirement in November 2014, less than two months after he was charged in connection with the shooting, and opted to take an immediate, lump-sum pension payout. He was allowed to keep the money, which according to current commissary price lists, could buy an abundance of snacks and supplies from the prison commissary during his stay at the Oklahoma State Penitentiary.[107]

During the three-year Kepler saga, Judge Holmes was also juggling other cases that cast a harsh light on Tulsa law enforcement.

Malcolm Scott and De'Marchoe Carpenter were 17 in 1994 when Tulsa cops arrested them in connection with a drive-by shooting that killed 19-year-old Karen Summers, the young mother of a 4-month-old baby.[108] The two men, both black, were each sentenced to life plus 170 years for first-degree murder. Two more black men "doing what blacks do," the public surmised.

The only problem was that they were innocent.

In 2005, Eric Cullen, a private investigator and then Director of the Oklahoma Innocence Project, received a letter from Scott in prison pleading for his help. Cullen worked to track down the witnesses, who recanted their statements. After 22 years in prison for a murder they didn't commit, in May, 2016, it was revealed that the police and the DA had withheld evidence during their 1995 trial that could have exonerated them.

The evidence included sworn statements from three rival gang members who claimed to be the actual perpetrators of the drive-by shooting. It also included signed affidavits from eyewitnesses recanting their testimony at trial. They said that Tulsa police detectives threatened them with murder charges if they didn't point the finger at Scott and Carpenter, and that the cops would record "only the rehearsed, coerced" portions of those interviews in police reports.

It was later revealed that detectives had visited the actual killer, 20-year-old Michael Lee Wilson, one day after the shooting. They found Wilson with the murder weapon and the getaway vehicle, and yet they released him after he agreed to testify against Carpenter and Scott. While he was out, Wilson went on to brutally murder a 30-year-old father and night clerk at a convenience store. Just before he was executed in 2014, he confessed that he, not Scott or Carpenter, had fired the shots that killed Karen Summers. In his videotaped confession two days before his death, he said, "All I know is I had the murder weapon on me and they let me go."[109]

Scott and Carpenter's exoneration was only one of the many cases reversed as a result of evidence of police corruption. A 2010 grand jury investigation of police corruption in Tulsa law enforcement resulted in 11 people being released from federal prison or having their cases dismissed due to evidence that they were framed by police officers.

Scott's older brother, Corey Atchison, had also been serving a life sentence. At the time his brother was exonerated, Atchison had already spent 28 years behind bars for a murder he repeatedly said he didn't commit. Atchison was convicted in 1991 through evidence his attorney said was obtained by the "coercion of a few scared kids," witnesses who were 15 and 17 years old at the time.[110]

After 22 years in prison for a murder they didn't commit, in May 2016, based on evidence never presented to the jury by police and then-DA Tim Harris in 1995, Judge Holmes declared them "actually innocent."

Two witnesses had recanted their testimony even before Atchison went to trial, and the prosecution's only star witness later recanted his identification of Atchison as the shooter, saying detectives and Assistant DA Tim Harris "threatened him with prison time" in 2000 if he told anyone 'the wrong man was in prison.'"[111] Multiple witnesses at the crime scene had identified the shooter to be someone other than Atchison, but they were never called to testify.[112]

After hearing from Malcolm Scott about his brother's similar plight, investigator Eric Cullen then assisted in exposing a similar pattern of witness coercion in Atchison's 1991 conviction. In 2019, based on the new revelations, Judge Holmes also vacated Atchison's murder conviction, which she called a "fundamental miscarriage of justice." She said that she was very concerned about the tactics used by law enforcement to interrogate the two teenagers. "Franky, I tell you, I was appalled at the way those interviews went," she said during proceedings. Like Scott and Carpenter before him, in July, 2019, Atchison walked out of the Tulsa County Jail a free man.

Former DA Tim Harris, who originally took Atchison's case to trial in 1991, disagreed with Holmes's decision, saying he had no issue with the police "tactics" used to secure witness testimony. After Atchison's release, current DA Kunzweiler, whom Harris hired in 2002 as an Assistant DA, released a statement defending Harris's actions in the case, stating that voters had repeatedly reelected Harris "because he embodied integrity."

After his brother's exoneration, Malcolm Scott sued the city of Tulsa and the detectives who set him up, alleging that Tulsa police fabricated evidence, failed to investigate leads, and coerced confessions to send at least seven other innocent people to prison. The officers denied the charges and sought to have the case dismissed. In the meantime, one of the detectives charged, Sergeant Mike Huff, was inducted into the 2019 Oklahoma Law Enforcement Museum and Hall of Fame.[113]

Scott's estimate of seven wrongfully convicted people turned out to be decidedly low. In the end, nearly 50 people had their sentences overturned or shortened in the wake of the corruption scandal.[114]

Eleven Tulsa police officers were indicted. Of those, three high-ranking Tulsa police officers—Jeff Henderson, J.J. Gray, and Harold Wells—and ATF Special Agent Brian McFadden—were convicted of falsifying search warrants, naming nonexistent informants, and giving false testimony. Two were charged with possession of crack cocaine with intent to distribute and conspiracy to steal money. The four officers received sentences that together totaled 187 months—over 15 years—in prison.

One of the many convictions overturned as a result of the police corruption was that of Larita Laird, a single mother sentenced in

2007 to 20 years in prison on evidence fabricated by the same officers. Laird, 43, spent nearly two years behind bars.

A search warrant by Tulsa police falsely claimed an informant purchased methamphetamine from Laird. The informant, it turned out, had also been coerced by Tulsa police officer Jeff Henderson, who had planted drugs in a toolbox in the informant's garage and then threatened, "We're going to take your kid, we're going to take your car, and you're going to prison" if he didn't agree to testify against Laird in their phony drug buy.

The scheme, extravagant and insidious as it was, succeeded in getting Laird indicted for possession of methamphetamine with intent to distribute, and in 2007 she received two ten-year prison sentences.

Unable to bond out of jail because the bonds were too high, Laird was shuttled from a federal prison in Texas through several prison and jail facilities across Oklahoma. She endured countless humiliating "bend over and cough" naked searches while lined up with other women. She was shackled to others and endured restrictions on feminine products, clothing, phone time, and contact with loved ones. She worked in a prison washroom and as a butcher in food services and would be off work by noon each day, but she was not allowed to shower the blood or debris from the butcher job off until that night because of the restricted shower hours. As a result, she would go to dinner hours later in bloody clothes from her job.[115]

At the time Laird was convicted, she had five children, the youngest a baby girl only four months old. She also had three other daughters, four, fourteen, and sixteen, and an eight-year-old son, who was killed while she was incarcerated by a drunk driver after getting off a school bus. When Laird asked the warden at the correctional center for permission to attend the funeral, the warden said not only, "No" but, "Heck no." He said she should have thought about that and been a better mother by not selling drugs in the first place."[116] For her constant crying, the prison psychologist and doctor gave her Prozac.

She was released in 2009 at the request of a federal special prosecutor after learning the charges were bogus and part of the larger conspiracy by Tulsa police to fabricate drug evidence. Brian McFadden, the ATF federal officer later convicted, had worked directly with Tulsa police Gang Unit and Special Investigations Division. Laird was falsely prosecuted on methamphetamine charges. Per the U.S. Attorney prosecuting the case, Officer McFadden said the only reason he went along with the prosecution of Laird was because "he had to carry it out to keep the charade going."[117]

When Laird returned home from prison, her youngest child didn't recognize her as her mom, and her second child was calling someone else mommy.

In 2012, she sued the city of Tulsa and the federal government. Without waiting for news of her $5 million award, she packed her family and moved away from Tulsa to a town where she said she is not afraid of the police.[118]

Laird's case was only the tip of the corruption iceberg in Tulsa law enforcement.

In 1995, Sedrick Courtney was sentenced to 30 years on robbery and burglary charges based on evidence that, he said, was planted by police. Police claimed the evidence had been destroyed. He was released after 16 years in prison when the Oklahoma Innocence Project recovered the evidence. Courtney filed a federal suit against the city in 2014 and received an $8 million settlement with the city of Tulsa.

Jeff Williams was released in 2016 after spending 17 years in a prison for manufacturing large amounts of methamphetamine, a crime he said he didn't commit. "I told the judge when I was sentenced that I didn't even know one of the people who said I had a lot of drugs," Williams said. A federal judge ruled that Tulsa police officers involved in the case — including several later convicted— manufactured evidence in order to secure his conviction and conducted an unconstitutional search and seizure the day he was arrested.

In a more notable travesty of justice, in 1995 17-year-old Michelle Murphy was sentenced to life without parole for stabbing her infant son to death. In 2014, a judge vacated her conviction and freed her after she had been incarcerated for 20 years, noting that Tulsa DA Tim Harris and Tulsa police had falsely claimed that unknown blood found at the scene was Murphy's. Harris had told the jury that blood evidence at the scene proved "beyond a reasonable doubt that [Murphy] murdered her son." In 2014 several independent lab tests proved that Michelle was not the murderer. Harris, who had since retired, said he "misspoke."

While Miashah's case was incidental to these, she was nonetheless a victim of the long-standing implicit bias in the Tulsa law enforcement and criminal justice system that had for decades derived low-level, primarily black, defendants of fair and just treatment under the law.[119]

In Miashah's case, the evidence she had never seen, provided by two electrical contractors who were never seriously considered by DeMier or allowed to testify, would likely have exonerated her at trial. Like many women before her, years of jail time in the knee-jerk circus of Tulsa's criminal justice system had cured her of any basic trust in the law.

Included in evidence reportedly gathered against Miashah was a package of marijuana allegedly found in a closet of Miashah's apartment after the fire. Chrisandria scoffed. "Oh sure, you mean the whole apartment burned up but the weed didn't?"

While it's difficult to know in retrospect, the possibility remains that if Sharon Holmes's powerful defense tactics had not been derailed by her election to the bench, Miashah's future might have turned out very different.

*

42

Crooked-ass cops

WITH Judge Holmes's re-election in 2018 came the re-election of another equally forceful voice for social justice.

Tulsa City Councilor Vanessa Hall-Harper, the council's only black member, was an outspoken advocate for District 1. She had butted heads with the Tulsa Police Department since her election in 2016 and was adamantly against what she saw as police corruption. She drew the ire of the police union following the acquittal of Police Officer Betty Shelby for shooting an unarmed black man when she called Shelby and the police officers who supported her "crooked-ass cops."

The comment drew retaliation from the police, who said her anti-police rhetoric was contributing to the wedge between law enforcement and community relations. They threatened to recruit a candidate to defeat her in the next election. Hall-Harper insisted her comments did not contribute to any anti-police sentiments. "I back the blue, but I back the good blue, not the crooked blue," she said. She went on to describe the Tulsa Police Department as "a culture of corruption."

The Shelby shooting drew national attention in September, 2016, when a police helicopter streamed live coverage of Officer Shelby, who was white, gunning down a heavy-set black man in the middle of a lonely street in north Tulsa. Terrence Crutcher, 40, was on his way to a community college class when his SUV suddenly stalled, blocking traffic. Shelby was on her way to another call when she came across Crutcher standing outside his stalled SUV across the center line. She was immediately suspicious of his behavior.

"Hey man, is this your vehicle?" she yelled.

When Crutcher didn't answer, she drew her gun and ordered him put his hands in the air. Crutcher complied and began walking toward Shelby, hands raised. He then reached in his left pocket as if searching for something, turned around, and began walking back toward his SUV, hands again raised.

"Get on your knees!" Shelby shouted, moving slowly toward him.

Circling overhead in the police helicopter, officers could be heard conversing with each other: "That looks like a bad dude… could be on something." Seated next to him in the helicopter was Betty Shelby's husband, Officer David Shelby.

As Crutcher neared his car, a second officer arrived on the scene. By this time, Crutcher was next to his car door and turned toward the police officers as if to reach inside the driver's window. As Shelby tightened her grip on her revolver, the second officer came up directly behind her left shoulder, Taser drawn, and shouted, "Taser!" Shelby, now roughly ten feet away, unleashed two rounds into Crutcher's chest and through his heart. Crutcher gasped, his hand against the car window, and slid to the ground, leaving a swath of blood on his partially open car window.

Under later query, Shelby said she fired in self-defense, fearing Crutcher was reaching into his vehicle for a weapon. No weapon was recovered from the SUV or his body. Laying on the dashboard near the window was Crutcher's wallet. The medical examiner determined he was blind in his right eye and deaf in his left ear. He may not have heard Shelby's commands over the din of the helicopter.

Less than a week later, Shelby was charged with first-degree manslaughter, a crime punishable with at least four years in prison. During her May, 2017, trial, jurors watched an hour-long video interview of Shelby in a dramatic performance during which a distraught Shelby alternated between sobbing, screaming, and sitting on the floor weeping, appearing emotionally drained.

During the trial, Corporal Marshall Eldridge, who taught the drug recognition courses to Tulsa police officers, testified on Shelby's training to determine whether a person was under the influence of drugs, and what kind. Eldridge testified that Shelby got a "zero" on a pop quiz because her answers were wrong. She then began "screaming and yelling and teared up" when she did poorly on the quiz, he said. She left the class of 24 officers and didn't return until someone went after her to talk her down.[120]

As the trial proceeded, an unspoken undertone of racism pervaded the atmosphere, though it was barely mentioned. Outside the courtroom, however, the national spectacle permeated every social media platform, national airway, and dining room table conversation across the country.[121] Hillary Clinton weighed in during a radio interview calling the scene "unbearable," adding such incidents "must be intolerable."[122]

It came as no surprise to the black community when a verdict of "Not Guilty" was delivered by a jury of ten white jurors and two black jurors. Protests erupted and racial sensitivities escalated. To the black community, the case was yet, the case was yet another example of a police officer shooting an unarmed black citizen. The case intensified the debate over race and policing in Tulsa.

Prosecutors maintained that Shelby got special treatment after she shot and killed Crutcher because she was a police officer. One of the 12 jurors who acquitted Shelby later penned a letter to Police Chief Chuck Jordan, saying that Shelby should never again be a patrol officer. He said the jury felt the state's prosecution "was shoddy" and that they could have gotten a conviction "had they done a better job."

Terrence Crutcher's twin sister, Tiffany Crutcher, was an attorney and former classmate of Vanessa Hall-Harper, who also had a twin brother. Tiffany took strong exception to the helicopter officer's characterization of her brother by police in the helicopter as a "bad dude."[123]

"That big 'bad dude' was my twin brother," she said. "That big 'bad dude' was a father. That big 'bad dude' was a son. That big 'bad dude' was enrolled at Tulsa Community College—just wanting to make us proud. That big 'bad dude' loved God. That big 'bad dude' was at church singing, with all his flaws, every week," she said.

Her comments resonated across the cultural landscape. Since Crutcher apparently wasn't doing anything wrong at the time, the helicopter officer's remarks clearly demonstrated racial bias—the kind that leads police to shoot and kill unarmed black men.[124] At the trial, when the police supervisor on duty the day of the shooting was asked if he thought race was a factor, he answered, "Yes, because of the mood and tone of America."[125]

After her acquittal, Shelby was relegated to a desk job in the Tulsa Police Department, which she openly detested. She resigned two months later to accept a position as an unpaid reserve deputy in a nearby Sheriff's Department, where she joined another former Tulsa police officer, Wayne Brown, terminated for posting racist social media posts on Facebook in support of waterboarding and anti-Islamic sentiments.[126]

In spite of Tulsa police union threats to mount a coalition to defeat Hall-Harper in her next election, she was reelected in 2018 with strong support from her northern district.

*

Controversy surrounding the Crutcher shooting was still circulating in 2018 when the Tulsa Equality Indicators Report was released, confirming what citizens in Hall-Harper's district had been saying for years.

The report measured social and economic equalities in the metropolitan area, such as education, gender, and housing, as compared to other U.S. cities of equal size. But it was the findings related to "Race and Officer Use of Force" that elicited the strongest reaction from the public.

> Blacks are five times more likely to be victims of officer use of excessive force than Hispanics, and whites as half as likely to experience use of force by police than blacks. Black adults are arrested more than twice as often as white adults in Tulsa,

> and black children are arrested more than three times as often as white children.[127]

The numbers were strongly disputed by the Tulsa Fraternal Order of Police (FOP), which argued that the methodology used to determine them was flawed, and that, in fact, African Americans are no more likely to be subject to use of force than any other race.[128]

Former city councilor G.T. Bynum had been elected mayor of Tulsa in 2016, and in light of the racial disparities noted in the Equality Report, he proposed the creation of an Independent Oversight Monitor to follow up on citizen complaints and review police investigations on use of force. It was immediately rejected by the FOP, noting that its union agreement prohibits changes to policy not previously agreed to by them, which meant, in essence, that they could operate with impunity under rules of their own making.

Councilor Hall-Harper, along with an activist group backed by the NAACP, demanded public hearings to address the stark racial disparities in the report. Her demand was immediately met with pushback from City Attorney David O'Melia, who insisted that Hall-Harper should not participate in hearings on police use of force because her husband, Sgt. Marcus Harper, was a police officer, creating a "conflict of interest."

Sgt. Marcus Harper was a homicide detective in the Tulsa Police Department Major Crimes Unit and president of the Tulsa's Black Officers Coalition, which had come out in support of an Independent Oversight Monitor proposed by the mayor to oversee police investigations and use of force. The police union, of which Marcus Harper ironically was himself a member, objected, stating that the union would sue the city if the mayor tried to implement the oversight program without the union's involvement.

Councilor Hall-Harper strongly denied a conflict of interest, but she was overridden by rest of the council, all white, who voted 7 to 1 to exclude her from the hearings.

Although the vociferous black councilwoman was viewed by some officials as a nuisance, she was a force to be reckoned with. A well-educated, strong-willed woman with a Bachelor's Degree in Political Science and a Master's in Management Science, she had spent 25 years in the Tulsa County Department of Health and the Juvenile Bureau, the same length of time she had been married to Marcus Harper. More importantly, the citizens of her district loved her.

As the city council prepared to move forward with public hearings into racial disparities, City Attorney O'Melia once again attempted to impede Hall-Harper's participation by way of a confidential memo to city councilors advising them to exclude Hall-Harper from the meetings. The memo again cited her marriage to a police officer as a conflict of interest. Many viewed this as yet another veiled attempt by city officials to suppress black voices. Hall-Harper again denied a conflict of interest, arguing that the hearings would not directly benefit her, but would benefit her community.

The dynamic of the discussion changed when four new city councilors were sworn in December 2018 and started pushing for it. "When a white person says it, then all of a sudden it's critical," Hall-Harper said. "As long as I was the only one at the table asking for it, it wasn't critical" adding, "That's just the fact."

The council voted in her favor, and in early 2019, four public hearings took place at various locations throughout the city with Hall-

Harper in attendance. The hearings created an unexpected blowback when a number of vocal residents, primarily black, appeared on live television and lambasted the panel with personal descriptions of questionable police conduct.

Animosity between the Tulsa police and Hall-Harper continued to grow, and by March, 2019, the fractious divide between the councilwoman and the Tulsa police union had evolved into a public standoff. The dispute came to a head one night when police dispatch received a 911 call about a stabbing in a north Tulsa home.

*

The call came in at 8:00 p.m. on March 2, 2019. Officers arrived to find Judge Sharon Holmes in her kitchen lying unconscious on the floor between the sink and kitchen island surrounded by blood. Her adult daughter, Adrienne, claimed she found her mother unresponsive on the kitchen floor with a kitchen knife buried in the back of her leg and had "slap-struck" her several times to revive her. Adrienne admitted the two had been arguing but denied it was physical and said her mother "fell on the knife." Her first call was to Sergeant Marcus Harper on his cell phone to report the alarming scene. Harper then called 911 and officers were dispatched to the home.

It was clear from the police report that the officer who took the report was skeptical:

> There was a large amount of blood pooled on the ground where she was laying, blood spatter on the bottom kitchen cabinets, and more blood pooled on the ground around the north side of

> the island countertop. There was a large kitchen knife in the sink that appeared to have blood on the blade, and the water was running from the tap in the sink.

Several officers were already in the house when Sergeant Harper arrived. The scene was chaotic. Adrienne was intermittently hysterical and resisted officers' attempts to determine what happened. Considering Holmes's position as a judge—and reluctant to jump to a conclusion—Sergeant Harper advised the reporting officer to title the incident an "accidental injury" until they could get more clarity from doctors' reports. Adrienne was unable to explain how her mother's ankle got broken.

One week later, Holmes implicated her daughter and Adrienne was charged with domestic assault and battery with a dangerous weapon. As a result, the Police Department launched an internal investigation into Sergeant Harper's instruction to designate the report an "accidental injury."

The hostile rhetoric boiled over into heated barbs between police and Vanessa Hall-Harper, who felt the department was turning against her husband, hoping to strong-arm her into shutting up. "It won't work," she said.

"Hall-Harper's unfounded accusations have no basis in fact," Police Chief Chuck Jordan responded.[129]

The final determination of who said what to whom at the scene of the stabbing was unclear, since police body cameras were muted, and the body camera footage of that portion had been completely blurred out.

In Tulsa, with its tortured racial history, old wounds reopen easily. Vitriolic public posts exposed sentiments still smoldering in the ruins of Black Wall Street:

"Trouble in paradise for the coons of Tulsa!" quipped one reader sarcastically.

"Typical violence, typical lying… from an absolutely lost element of our society," echoed another.

A decision on the Independent Oversight Monitor was tabled when the police union demanded that terms be settled in accordance with its union agreement. However, results of the open meetings placed a harsh focus on the need for more transparency in police interactions with the public.

Sgt. Harper was cleared and returned to duty.[130] After a short recovery, in July, 2019, Judge Holmes returned to the bench on crutches in time to free Corey Atchison from a life sentence for a murder he didn't commit.

*

Controversy surrounding the stabbing still simmered in late 2019 when Chrisandria settled back in Tulsa with her family. She had worked closely with Sharon Holmes when she was Miashah's defense attorney before her election to the bench and was shocked to learn of the assault on Holmes by the judge's own daughter. "*What child could do that to her mother?*" she asked herself. This raised yet another nagging question that had lingered in Chrisandria's mind since Miashah's arrest: "*Who could do this to my child?*"

It was answered one afternoon in a most unconventional way at a strip mall in midtown Tulsa. For Chrisandria, the chance encounter was as difficult to foresee as it was to forget. She said, "I was at the thrift store and right next door is a store where they fix phones. I'm just standin' there smokin' a cigarette and a couple of black guys were there talking to each other. And one said, 'You know I can't work like that anymore. I'm a different man now. I'm older. I have to do God's work. This is an evil place. These crackers, they're devils.'"

Then, Chrisandria heard, "You know the little girls that got killed?"

She said, "Immediately my mind goes to say, 'That was me! Those were my granddaughters!' But somethin' in me said, 'Shut up and listen.' And like it was a miracle. He said, 'You know, I'm a police officer… I worked on that case during that time and the way they booked that black female—they knew they were wrong. They knew they had evidence that she didn't do that.'"

Chrisandria remembered, "It was weird, you know, when something like that happens, you question yourself: 'Am I just trippin?' And the guy was sayin', 'I want to tell you how racist this place is. And how much racism there is in the Police Department. And y'all need to stand with me.' He had been suspended pending an internal investigation. Now *he* was in trouble with the cops."

Chrisandria could no longer hold her tongue. "Stand with you?" she interrupted the conversation. "Now you want somebody to stand with you? Brother, brother, you were not for the people when they arrested Miashah. It was you that was being abusive to a little 5-foot-tall female. You was talkin' bad shit, bad shit—turnin' it up for the white people, doin' the dance! I remember when this happened and you were the house nigger! Now they threw your ass under the bus and you want us to stand with you!?"

For Chrisandria, it was yet another part of the biased criminal justice system that ripped her family apart. And in her mind, it went far beyond Miashah. It applied to part of a painful past seldom mentioned in the Moses family. A cold case swept under the rug—or, more accurately, under the water. As if maybe, just maybe, like stories of the 1921 Race Massacre, if you don't talk about it, it didn't really happen.

43

Cold case

IT was a blip in the headlines. A flash in the Tulsa newspaper one day, and again, three days later. And then, gone. The year was 1987.

Thirty years later, Tulsa Police Department reports, Tulsa Fire Department records, and even the smallest shred of evidence of the incident are nowhere to be found. The north Tulsa funeral home that buried him had long since been abandoned, and the guard at the upscale gated complex where his body was found developed dementia and died.

But then he was just another black boy. What was he doing there anyway? And did anybody care?

Earleen Simmons cared. The boy's mother had been searching for her missing son for two months after he walked out the door that night in November, 1986, and never came back. Repeated calls to the Tulsa Police Department over the next two months to report a missing person were to no avail. Maybe he ran off, they said, making it clear it would interfere with their time in tracking down other missing people.

Then came the headline on February 1, 1987:

"Ice Hides Body in Condominium Pond"[131]

His name appeared in the paper as Hose Simmons, Jr., but nobody ever called him that. He was "Junior" to his mom and siblings. His dad, Hose Sr., was the only one they knew by that name. His three best friends in the neighborhood, Truman, Craig, and Marvin, never knew him by that name either. To them, he was simply Junior. To his little sister, Chrisandria, he was the ever-pesky big brother.

"I love you, sis," he teased that night when he came through the back door behind her, twisting her hair. It was 10 o'clock at night. Her mom Earleen was already in bed asleep before her 1:00 a.m. shift at a local hotel, leaving Chrisandria, 12, and her little sister, Shelia, 11, to do the dishes. Junior tossed his jacket on his bed and headed back out through the garage. The garage door was up and Chrisandria watched through the screen door as he left. He gave a quick nod to his little brother Robin, 18, who was sitting in a car at the curb drinking beer with a friend. He then jumped into a car with Truman and Marvin and vanished into the night.

It was the last time anyone in the family ever saw him alive.

Earleen, a 5-foot, petite woman, was the undisputed matriarch of the family and kept tabs on her kids as best she could. By now, a good foot shorter than her eldest son Junior, she nevertheless maintained her role as the gatekeeper of those who came and went in the small house.

"Junior was a quiet kid, kind of restrained," Earleen said. "He had graduated from high school and lived at home. And he had his little friends—like guys have—that he liked to run around with.

He'd just turned 20. And when they're over 18, you know, you can't monitor them." She remembers hearing him come through the back door that night. "I could hear his feet going through the hallway. I could hear the girls in the kitchen washing the dishes and kidding, you know how kids do. And I heard, 'Quit it, Junior!' And then he was gone."

It was the Tuesday before Thanksgiving. Earleen worried for weeks. She called all the surrounding jails. She even drove to Arizona where her mother lived, thinking maybe he caught a ride there.

Thanksgiving came with no word. "The atmosphere was deathly quiet around the Thanksgiving table, 'cause mama fixed all this dinner and Junior didn't come," Chrisandria said. Then Christmas came, still no Junior.

Chrisandria was a young, impressionable girl in grade school when Junior went missing and started to have strange dreams. Once, in the middle of the night, she woke her mother up and said, "Junior put his hands on me, and they were wet. And I was too scared to turn around to look."

"She was shaking," Earleen said. "And that was before they ever found his body in the lake."

Earleen was having premonitions of her own: "Junior came to me one night, and he kept walkin' and walkin', and I was tryin' to catch up with him. And I said, 'Junior, what happened to you?' And he just kept walkin' and never turned around. Finally, he said, 'Mama, I can't tell you that.' And I woke up with my face wet with tears."

Still, she clung to hope that he would walk back through the door—that he would surely call.

"Every time the phone rang my heart would jump," Earleen said. "I never heard from him again, ever in my life. The next time I heard about him, he was dead."

His body was found in an inlet of a small man-made lake. The police said his body floated to the top under the ice of a pond in South Shore Condominiums, an upscale living complex in midtown Tulsa. "Some kids saw it through the ice and thought it was a dog because it was January and it had froze," Earleen said. "And when it finally got warm enough, it popped up."

The main lake at the center of the complex was surrounded by five narrow canals, all frozen solid that winter. The detectives who came to Earleen's house to deliver the news said Junior was cut around his ankles and whoever threw him in evidently thought they had killed him. News reports said it looked like he'd been thrown over the side of a condo on the lake and floated through a canal.

But the police didn't tell her about the big abrasion over his left eye. A fireman told her about it a month after Junior was buried. Her white next-door neighbor had called and said a fireman who lived down the street said he was the one who pulled Junior out of the pond. Earleen knew the fireman's house and knocked on his door.

"I'm the one who pulled the body out," he said. "And he had a big abrasion over his left eye. Like somebody hit him."

"Will you testify to that?" Earleen asked.

"No, no. I can't get involved with all of this," he answered.

The coroner told Earleen that Junior had water in his lungs and had likely drowned. He said it looked like he was trying to get out of something and tore his feet up. The "type of death" was listed as "violent or unnatural," and the "manner of death" was marked "unknown." Earleen never actually saw her son's body. "I couldn't stand to look at my baby," she said. Two weeks later, the family held a closed-casket funeral.

Police theorized Junior tried to swim across the main lake and got his feet tangled up in something and drowned. But Earleen wasn't having it. The temperature that Thanksgiving was near freezing. "No, my son don't go swimmin' in November!" she said. "My son don't go swimmin' in November 'cause he had only a muscle shirt on and his billfold was found on him in the water. *I don't even know any black people who go swimmin' in the winter!*"

It was ludicrous to his little brother Robin, too. "*My brother hated water. Period. He hated water.*" He said Junior had taken his shirt off, something he would never do unless he was going to whip somebody. "Everybody was acting real nervous," he said. "And the firefighter who pulled him out was terrified. Like somethin' bad had happened."[132]

With this, Earleen went back downtown to talk to the lead detective.

"You know that and I know that," the detective said. "That he didn't go swimming."

"Yeah, I know that," she nodded.

"There's a lot of unsolved cases here in Tulsa, and here's the notebooks to prove it," the detective said, pointing to a pile of notebooks in his office. The stack of notebooks would have reached her chin.

"These are the unsolved cases here in Tulsa. Do you have money to put up a reward?"

"No sir, I do not, sir. I don't have no money," she said.

"Then you'll never know what happened to your son. That's what happens here."

The police offered no further explanation—but the family in the small house on North Boulder Avenue had their own ideas.

Earleen Simmons had raised three sons and three daughters with her husband Hose Simmons, Sr., before the marriage went by the wayside. Later, she met Robert Lee Moses and set about raising three more daughters, including Chrisandria. She had nine children. The frame house was small but adequate for her growing family.

But money was hard to come by, and the family struggled to pay their electric bills. It was around this time that Junior and his young teenage friends began spending time across the street in the house of Jimmy Mack, a black firefighter. Sometimes Jimmy would take them on outings, swimming, basketball. Sometimes they would go to a black preacher's house across the tracks, and for whatever reason, they always came home with money. The two men liked having the young boys around, and the boys needed the money, so the arrangement seemed fair. They were just kids, after all, and didn't care. It meant heat in the house and maybe a pair of new sneakers for school.

As time went on, the boys spent more and more time at Jimmy Mack's house. Chrisandria knew who he was because she saw him get up early in the mornings to head to the fire station.

"But he was strange," Earleen said. "He would make cakes for the boys and give them money, and I didn't like that. He would give the other boys money too. I mean, he didn't act normal."

She had an inkling something was odd but didn't think much of it until her younger son Robin came running in the house one day. He'd been to Jimmy Mack's.

"Mama, that sucker asked me to kiss him," he said. "And I took off runnin'. I ain't never goin' down there anymore. He's a weirdo."

"Huh?" Earleen asked, just coming in from work.

"He cooked Junior a cake for his birthday," he said.

When Junior came in that afternoon, she warned him to stay away from the place.

"But Mama, there's nothin' to fret about," he argued. "Craig and all of them go down to Jimmy's house. They're always going there!"

For his part, Robin wasn't going back. "He's a weirdo," he said. "And the preacher's a weirdo too." Eventually, the preacher moved across town, but Truman and the boys would drive there.

Such was life in the neighborhood in the 1980s.

By 1986, the preacher had moved to South Shore Condominiums, a luxury condo in a private gated complex across the street from Tulsa's elite Southern Hills Country Club, site of PGA golf championships attended by notables such as astronaut Neil Armstrong and golf greats Phil Michelson and Tiger Woods. South Shore was a sprawling complex with an array of two-story condos, each overlooking a scenic main lake with fountains and a walkway to a club house in the center of the lake. More condos spanned either side of the five narrow canals that ran through the complex. The preacher's condo was on the far north end of a canal with a spacious roped deck overlooking a quiet inlet.

Jan, the manager of the condo, said parties at the condo were sometimes loud, and she thought the preacher who lived there was some sort of musician. The gated entrance was attended 24 hours a day, and only guests approved by a resident were admitted through the gate. Carol Rose was the guard on the evening shift and remembered the boys coming through the gate in a car late that night.

What happened after that was anybody's guess.

No police reports could be found to explain the disturbance at the condominiums on November 25, 1986. Nor was there a record of the police car Carol Rose saw coming through the gate, then leaving with a black kid in the back seat and returning later with the same black kid. When the police car left the last time, he wasn't in it.

Carol Rose never saw him again—nor did any of the other boys.

When he was pulled from the icy waters, Junior still had his wallet in his back pocket. After his body was identified, a police detective took a picture of Hose to the South Shore security office and showed it to Carol Rose.

"Yeah, I saw that guy go in with some other boys to the reverend's apartment that night," she said. "And what they were doing there, I don't know."

The detective then circled around to the preacher's condo and showed him the photo. The preacher said he didn't know any Hose and didn't know how his name got on his visitor list. The detective then went back to Carol Rose, who insisted that was the only way he could have been admitted. She found two names on the list: Junior and Craig.

None of the Junior's neighborhood friends ever talked about what happened that night. "In the neighborhood you have codes,"

Robin said. "There's certain things you don't talk about. In the hood, nobody is as buddy-buddy as you think."

Truman was with Junior that night but didn't speak about it for years. Neither did Marvin or Craig. In the years since Hose's disappearance, they had all moved on with their lives—gotten married, had kids, or had run-ins with the law. Everyone lost track of everyone else.

Robin heard rumors about it from friends, but nobody would ever tell him what happened. It was twenty-plus years before he ran into Truman and he finally opened up about it. Earleen remembered what Robin told her about it: "It was that old preacher that allowed things to mess up," Truman said. "When the police came, we ran, and Junior ran the wrong way and ran right into the police. We peeked out, and the police had him layin' on the ground. And then we really took off. We thought they took him to jail, but they didn't. They didn't take him to jail."[133] According to Robin, Truman never spoke of it again.

The temperature that Thanksgiving was near freezing, yet news reports said Hose drowned "while deliberately trying to swim across the lake and his body had floated into a canal." But South Shore residents said the lake was less than four feet deep. Junior was six feet tall and could have simply stood up. On top of that, it was not physically possible for a body to float from the main lake into the canal where Junior's body was found; during construction in 1974, barricades were built for streets inside the complex that blocked the main lake from the canals.

The question remains: Did he jump from a deck? *Or was he thrown in dead?*

Thirty years later, Earleen still has Junior's billfold with a wrinkled piece of paper in it with a girl's phone number. By then, the preacher had become a mega-star evangelist at a large church in south Tulsa with an overflowing congregation of Christian believers.

Although police spokesman Lt. Orndorff reported the drowning to the news media in January, 1987, Tulsa police could find no record of any such incident at South Shore Condominiums in November, 1986, nor could they find the report of a body being pulled from the lake, despite the medical examiner's notation that his body was delivered to them by the police. Nor could the Tulsa Fire Department find any record that a Jimmy Mack had ever worked there, though his then-wife Virginia said that he did. Lt. Orndorff has since passed away, as had the firefighter who recovered Junior's body from the canal.

The answer lies somewhere in the unwritten record of things best left untold.

But Junior's little brother suspects he knows the reason. "I know for a fact my brother was messin' with people who were gay or bi-sexual," Robin said, which he believes is the reason he hung around with Jimmy Mack and the preacher. "Something happened at South Shore that night, and the preacher had something to do with it," Robin said. "The police hid it because he was big in the community. They hid it." And the boys in the neighborhood gang hid it too. "When people are aware of a crime… They don't talk about it. Especially in the hood. It ain't as friendly as that."

The truth about what actually happened that night in 1986 is buried in the minds of a handful of north side boys—and in the body of a black kid who can never tell.

44

Ghosts of the past

TULSA Mayor G.T. Bynum's voice had a tone of stern resolve as he delivered his 2019 State of the City address:

"Be assured that the city will investigate every homicide within its borders… no matter how hard the way or challenging the case… no matter how much time has passed. If officials covered up an even greater crime than is reflected in death certificates, that only makes the onus all the greater on the city to pursue the issue today."[134]

The mayor's comments weren't referring to the case of Hose Simmons, Jr. He was referring to the long-awaited search for mass graves of the black men, women, and children reportedly carted off and buried in unidentified locations during the 1921 Tulsa Race Massacre.[135]

Earleen's sister Amanda still fumes at the memories of Junior's death and the massacre. The two horrors linger together in her mind.

"I tell you what, I was there when Junior went missing and I was there when they found his body. And they never investigated! The Tulsa Police did nothing to help my sister find her child!" she chafed. "All we know is that some kids found him. My sister had been looking for him. You can't find nothing on it! Like in Oklahoma when they dug those graves and built houses!" The two had parallels. Bodies disappearing with no record, both largely forgotten.

As with the bodies buried that infamous Memorial Day weekend in 1921, an unsavory part of Oklahoma history was buried—and a conspiracy of silence was born. Motivated by shame and a refusal to value the lives and property of the victims of the race massacre, Tulsa intentionally hid the story of the slaughter for decades, leaving it out of the history books and omitting it from school history classes. Accounts of the massacre were literally torn out of the first edition of the May 31, 1921 *Tulsa Tribune* newspaper as Tulsans tried to erase accounts, memories, and events of one of the darkest chapters in the history of American race relations.[136]

Vanessa Hall-Harper, whose council district included Greenwood, remembers her grandmother whispering to her before she died. "They was killing black people and running them out of the city." Hall-Harper said she didn't even know about the massacre until she was an adult. "And I was raised here. It wasn't taught about in the schools. It was taboo to speak about it."

Survivors recounted black bodies loaded on trucks and dumped off bridges into the Arkansas River. Some were seen floating southward by people in downstream towns.[137] Bodies of victims, referred to as negroes from "Little Africa," were reported far and wide, from the river to abandoned coal mines to distant fields.

"It was quite a trauma to find out people hated you for your color," Hall-Harper's grandmother told her.[138]

Rumors of mass graves circulated among citizens of Greenwood for decades but were ignored or dismissed by city officials, who balked at the proposition of an expensive anthropological search across several supposed burial sites.

Then, in 1999, a white man named Clyde Eddy, who was ten at the time of the massacre, came forward and told officials he was playing in Oaklawn Cemetery in 1921 when he saw white men digging a trench. When the men left, Eddy said, he peeked inside the wooden crates and saw the corpses of black people.

Based on Eddy's story, state archaeologists began to investigate the section of the cemetery Eddy cited. Using ground-penetrating radar, they made a dramatic discovery: an anomaly bearing "all the characteristics of a dug pit or trench with vertical walls and an undefined object within the approximate center of the feature. With Mr. Eddy's testimony, this trench-like feature takes on the properties of a mass grave."

But Oaklawn Cemetery is a public burial lot which now contained the graves of local families, possibly laid on top of the identified trench.[139] The Oklahoma Commission to Study the Tulsa Race Riot of 1921 created by the Oklahoma legislature in 1997 to establish a historical record of the massacre, recommended "a limited physical investigation of the feature be undertaken to clarify whether it indeed represents a mass grave."

But the investigation never happened. Then-mayor Susan Savage raised concerns about the excavation. "Oaklawn Cemetery is a public lot," Savage said. "How do we do that without disturbing graves of family buried there? "

With that, the question of mass graves was left an unresolved issue and excavation of Oak Lawn Cemetery was placed on hold.

The refusal to pursue legal alternatives for excavation of Oaklawn Cemetery was a blow to Hall-Harper, who claimed that

Greenwood history was being intentionally ignored. "They just want to forget about it and move on," she said.

Now, nearly one hundred years later, ghosts of the hidden past were rising up in the voices of Tulsa's north side citizens.

At the urging of Hall-Harper and advocates of the black community, Mayor Bynum finally agreed to undertake the controversial initiative, which included electromagnetic radar searches for bodies, bones, or anomalies in four locations, Newblock Park, which operated as a dump in 1921, Rolling Oaks Memorial Gardens, Oaklawn Cemetery, and The Canes, a small piece of land near the Arkansas River covered in overgrown vegetation. Those familiar with Mayor Bynum knew that he possessed the negotiating skills and fortitude required to take on the century-long controversy.

A Public Oversight Committee was established to oversee the search made up of descendants of victims of the massacre and current leaders in Tulsa's African American community.

But many black Tulsans remained suspicious of the city government. They felt that city institutions had systematically ignored and exploited them for the past century. At one point during a Public Oversight Committee meeting, committee member Rev. Robert Turner of the Vernon AME Church, one of the hallmark buildings in north Tulsa that was nearly burned to the ground, took exception to the inordinate delay in securing permission for excavation in Rolling Oaks Memorial Gardens. Turner, who is black said the city was just putting on a show. He then lay on the floor to represent the unrecovered remains of massacre victims.[140]

Determined to pinpoint the location for a reporter, Hall-Harper drove her black SUV down a gravel road in south Tulsa and came to a halt at a grassy knoll in the potter's field section of Oaklawn

Cemetery. "This is where the mass graves are," she said, pointing to the location where she believes bodies were dumped.

Mayor Bynum ultimately secured permission from Rolling Oaks Memorial Garden to proceed with excavation there and permission to conduct a test excavation of Oaklawn Cemetery. Two other sites with cursory results from a preliminary archaeological search found anomalies that called for additional surveying.

"There is a technical side of it, but more complex than the human dimension of it," Bynum said. But it's difficult to fathom after a hundred years of loss—lost ancestry, lost grieving, lost memories, lost funerals—how anything could be more humane than simply *knowing*.

45

Never-ending hourglass

EVIDENCE of the distrust that has been handed down through generations can be found even in the answers of small children when asked by a Tulsa school counselor what the job of a police officer is. At one school, answers included "to protect us" and "to get the bad guys." But in other schools, the answers were very different: "To take my dad to jail" and "to throw my brother to the ground and handcuff him for no reason." One little second-grade black boy gave an especially startling answer: "To kill us."[141] These answers are living proof that legacies from the past are still present in the minds of north side citizens.

Chrisandria, for one, witnessed the pain suffered by members of her own family by ingrained prejudices. "This whole atrocity is just draped in a big Ku Klux Klan hood over the whole state. The way we are treated…," she said. "They just dress it up here like it was in 1921. And by time the 80s and 90s came in, they've got to dress it up a different way. They basically just change the prejudice with the time. Like fashion changes. That's all they do."

Miashah and others like her are buried in modern Oklahoma's version of mass graves: rows of concrete crypts in catacombs of doom that hold the remains of lives gone astray and of women with little or no way out, delivered there on the conveyor belt of archaic criminal codes, unchecked officials, and misguided justice. Women are stuffed in overcrowded prisons with hardly room to breathe.

In a November 2018 interview, DA Kunzweiler said he likes to explain women's imprisonment using a metaphor about spankings. "Let's take a mother struggling with addiction, he said. Her first time getting caught, perhaps she deserves a lecture. If she relapses, she's due for a grounding—some jail time. But if she continues to get in trouble? The consequences of any true disciplinary system must become dire," Kunzweiler said. Some cases require skipping the lecture and going right to the spanking. He smacked his hands together as if to resemble a spanking or slamming cell door.[142]

After the 10 o'clock news, the women pass out of the public domain and into the painfully quiet corners of the ordinary lives of the survivors.

"This is a cruel place," Chrisandria said, looking back at the misery that pervaded her family through the years. "People need to quit trying to dress it up and put a bow on it. This is a shitty-ass place," she said. As soon as Miashah gets out, Chrisandria plans to leave Oklahoma. "It's getting to the end now. I don't like it here. It's definitely not where I want to be, but I know it's something unfinished. So, I'm not leaving until whatever the Most High is havin' me do is done."

The full story of the Moses family is difficult to fathom, yet it is just one example of how thousands of other families have been trapped for centuries behind a silent wall of color. They remain burdened by challenges that few on the southside of the tracks with lighter skins understand any more than their forebears did a century ago when black people lay dying on those tracks.

A subtle thread of racial bias still lingers as the backdrop of everyday life in Tulsa, harbored by citizens of all ranks and positions. Some occupy prestigious mansions, some sit piously in church pews, and others have donned badges.

Meanwhile, an occasional billow of smoke is seen rising from midtown Tulsa over the London Square apartment complex.

Less than two years after the fire that destroyed Miashah's life, another fire erupted in the wall of apartment #723, directly across from Miashah's old unit. A call to the Tulsa Fire Department went out in the early morning hours of May, 2015. Firemen forced their way into the apartment and tore out the dry wall to extinguish the fire. The apartment was vacant at the time. The cause was listed as "Undetermined."

On July 31, 2018, the Tulsa Fire Department responded to another fire in London Square. Firefighters arrived to find flames shooting out a second-story window, lapping onto the roof. A mother and a child made it out unharmed. One unit was heavily damaged and two others were rendered uninhabitable due to smoke damage. The fire incident report noted it started from an "unknown source" in the living room of apartment #631 and burned through the attic. The cause of the fire was listed as "Undetermined."

Tulsa Fire Captain Larry Bowles noted that all London Square fires shared a common denominator: The buildings weren't equipped with automatic sprinkler systems. "This is damage that wouldn't have happened if an automatic sprinkler system was equipped in each building," Bowles said. "Automatic sprinkler systems do what they're supposed to do—help put out fires."

After Miashah's fire, construction contractors Famous Tankersley and Jack Palau pressed the complex owner, Paul Forkeotes, to install fire sprinklers. Forkeotes said he was adamant that they do not pursue sprinklers for Miashah's building during the repairs, because "his boilers were always having problems and he could not keep enough heat to prevent the sprinklers from freezing."

While Miashah's release is scheduled for 2022, one possibility remains: If on November 18, 2013, she had lived anywhere else besides London Square, she might have returned home after taking out the trash to find her nieces alive and happy, watching television right where she left them.

*

A cluster of dandelions springs through the cracks of the busted asphalt streets of Greenwood, as does a trace of revival spring through the broken lives of the Moses family. The first ray of hope came on November 13, 2017.

His name was "Nas," short for his grandfather Courtney's given name, Nasir. And the little guy was more than ready for his role, the mischievous embodiment of his two big sisters lost in the hellish fire in London Square. He most certainly knew them even before he arrived here on earth November 13, 2017. Almost four years to the day after Noni and Nylah ascended into heaven on a pillar of smoke—Keahmiee had a baby boy.

Courtney had been gone less than a year when Nas arrived, a pint-sized widget to take his place. Although no real blood relation to his namesake, he inexplicably looked like him. There had been no question in Keahmiee's mind what to call him.

Her stepdad Courtney was known by everyone as Courtney Fletcher, but his true name was Nasir Hassad. Courtney's father was an Ethiopian man, his mother African American. She later remarried a man with the last name of Fletcher and gave Courtney his last name. "But Courtney hated the name Fletcher, Chrisandria said. "He hated it."

Little Nas would surely have made Courtney smile. Hardly a patient child, the two-year old could get into things faster than his mother could get him out of them, his hair standing up in 4-inch baby dreadlocks, running into the coffee table with his toy red truck. He was a little man's man and certainly not prone to his sisters' female tendencies—except for Nylah's chubby smile when it lights up his face.

Miashah gets letters with pictures of the family and little Nas. "I can't believe my sister hasn't changed on me," she said. "God really knew that I wouldn't be able make it without my family. I'm a family person. I just thank God that they stood by me."

When the prison gates spring wide in 2022, Miashah will be greeted by her little sister Keahmiee and a happy toddler with Nylah's smile, eager to meet his "Auntie Moe."

*

Nas, 2 years old, in his 1921 Black Wall Street shirt. (Photo: Keahmiee Moses)

About the author

Carol Mersch is an Oklahoma author and journalist specializing in creative non-fiction. She has published six books and numerous articles which she authored and co-compiled with others in areas of space exploration, law enforcement, and spirituality.

Her close friendship with Apollo 14 astronaut Edgar Mitchell led her to develop *The Apostles of Apollo: The Journey of the Bibles to the Moon* (Pen-L Publishing, 2010), for which she was accepted into the Mayborn Literary Guild, and *The Space Less Traveled (*Pen-L Publishing, 2013*),* a book of quotations gleaned from her years of companionship with Mitchell. In 2013, her literary document *Religion, Space Exploration and Secular Society* was accepted by Taylor & Frances, a national consortium in the UK offering document subscription services used by museums, libraries, and universities, including the Smithsonian Air & Space Museum.

Prior to this, Mersch was instrumental in publishing several books, including *The Seamless Bible* (Destiny Image, 2004), a chronological presentation of the King James Bible and *The Seamless Gospels* (Destiny Inage, 2005), *Coming Home: For Those who Serve and Those who Wait* (Elm Hill Books, 2004), a devotional/journal for US troops, *Year of Promise (*iUniverse Publishing, 2011), 365-day devotional/journal, and *The Heart of a Cop*: *Stories of Personal Faith from the Line of Duty* (Clovercroft Publishing, 2016). Her latest book,

Undaunted: The Unflinching Faith, Audacity and Ultimate Betrayal of an American Legend (Pen-L Publishing), chronicling the life of ordained Presbyterian pastor and NASA Chaplain Reverend John Stout, was released in September 2019. Her book *We Are One* (Pen-L Publishing) chronicling the transformative experience of Apollo 14 Lunar Module Pilot Edgar Mitchell during his return from the moon is scheduled for release mid-2020.

In 2016, she authored an online long-form article *Trial by Fire* published in *The Big Round Table,* a platform supported by staff of the Columbia School of Journalism.

Before launching her writing career, she served at the executive level of several Fortune 1000 enterprises and at the helm of three privately held companies where she received local and national recognition for her contributions to community and civic endeavors.

Mersch has authored numerous articles for national trade and online publications on Information Technology and developed an IT strategy manual utilized by several leading corporations and local governments. She is a high-energy individual who brings integrity and success to any endeavor she undertakes. In 1999 her firm, Mersch-Bacher Associates, was awarded the Blue Star Award for entrepreneurship, and the success of Mersch and her company was featured on a nationally televised PBS special. In August 2000 *The New York Times* cited her work in community and civic endeavors.

In 2004, she left the corporate world to form ProvidenceWorks LLC, a business enterprise for developing articles and books "that make a difference." During this time, she authored, compiled, and co-complied numerous non-fictions works.

In 2011-2018 she was featured on Houston Fox26, Tulsa ABC NewsOn6, BBC World Radio, Dallas CBS Radio KRLD, MSNBC,

CNN Faith, and two magazines in Europe, *Spaceflight Magazine* and *Sorted*, a Christian men's magazine, for her research into the first Lunar Bible covered in her book *The Apostles of Apollo.* The historic Bibles carried to the moon and their heirship have been featured by the Associated Press, the *Houston Chron*icle, the *Baytown Sun,* MSNBC, Fox News, CNN Belief, and *Al Jazeera* "America Tonight" (Sept 2015). For more information see www.carolmersch.com,

Notes

1 Tulsa County Case CF-2013-5838 State of Oklahoma vs. Miashah Chantell Moses, Preliminary Hearing, Mar 13, 2014.

2 "Police Arrest Aunt of children Killed in Tulsa apartment Fire," NewsOn6, Dee Duren, Emory Bryan, Nov 19, 2103.

3 "Tulsa woman charged with death of nieces back in custody," Fox23, Angela Hong, Aug 13, 2014.

4 Mass Incarceration of Women and Minorities a New Crisis," *Insight News*, Stacy M. Brown, May 5, 2019.

5 "Why Oklahoma has the highest incarceration rate in the country," *Reveal*, Allison Herrera, Feb 13, 2019.

6 "States of Women's Incarceration: The Global Context 2018," *Prison Policy initiative*, Aleks Kaisture, June 2018

7 "America's other family-separation crisis," *New York Magazine*, Sarah Stillman, Nov 5, 2018.

8 "Unique Challenges Facing Women in the Criminal Justice System," Still She Rises Tulsa, 2019

9 Bureau of Justice Statistics, 2014

10 Centers for Disease Control's National Violence against Women Survey

11 Prison Rape Elimination Act Committee, 2014.

12 Bureau of Justice Statistics, 2012

13 "Female prison in Oklahoma highest rape rate in U.S." *The Oklahoman*, Graham Lee Brewer, Jan 12, 2014.

14 "Oklahoma's Mabel Bassett Correctional Center has Highest Prison Rape Rate," *Prison Legal News*, Mar 7, 2016.

15 "Prison rape hearing: Mabel Bassett officials decline to testify on issues at McCloud facility," *Tulsa World*, Graham Lee Brewer, Jan 12, 2014.

16 "Sexual Attacks Investigated at Oklahoma Women's Prison," Tulsa CBS NewsOn6, Lisa Monahan, Sep 2, 2014.

17 Madigan, Steve, "The Burning," Thomas Dunne Books, St. Martin's Griffin (2001) NY, New York.

18 "Black Wall Street: The African American Haven That Burned," *The Ringer*, Victor Luckerson, June 28, 2018.

19 Gates, Eddie Faye, "They Came Searching" (Eakin Press, Austin, TX, 1997).

20 Madigan, Steve, "The Burning" (Thomas Dunne Books: St. Martin's Griffin, NY, New York, 2001).

21 Ibid.

22 Madigan, Steve, "The Burning" (Thomas Dunne Books: St. Martin's Griffin, NY, New York, 2001).

23 Marsh, Corinda Pitts, "Holocaust in the Homeland: Black Wall Street's Last Days," Corinda Marsh, (2014).

24 Madigan, Steve, "The Burning," Thomas Dunne Books (St. Martin's Griffin, NY, New York, 2001).

25 "Black Wall Street: The African American Haven That Burned," *The Ringer*, Victor Luckerson, June 28, 2018.

26 "The Eruption of Tulsa," *The Nation*, Walter F. White, Jun 29, 1921.

27 "Tulsa Race Massacre: 1921 Tulsa newspapers fueled racism, and one story is cited for sparking Greenwood's burning," *Tulsa World*, Randy Krehbiel May 21, 2019.

28 Marsh, Corinda Pitts, "Holocaust in the Homeland: Black Wall Street's Last Days," Corinda Marsh (2014).

29 Ibid.

30 "A Long-Lost Manuscript Contains a Searing Eyewitness Account of the Tulsa Race Massacre of 1921," *Smithsonian Magazine*, Allison Keyes, May 27, 2016.

31 "Black Wall Street: The African American Haven That Burned," *The Ringer*, Victor Luckerson, June 28, 2018.

32 Tina Long, London Square tenant interview with author, June 25, 2016.

33 "Police Arrest Aunt of children Killed in Tulsa apartment Fire," NewsOn6, Dee Duren, Emory Bryan, Nov 19, 2103.

34 Tina Long, London Square tenant interview with author, June 25, 2016.

35 Ibid.

36 Jon Hodges, London Square Tenant interview with author, 12-29-15.

37 "London Square Fire Suspect Arrested," Tulsa Police Division overnight police report, Nov 14, 2013.

38 Tulsa Police Arrest Report CF-13-5838, Miashah Moses, 11-19-13

39 Tina Long, London Square tenant interview with author, June 25, 2016.

40 "Police Arrest Aunt of Children Killed in Tulsa Apartment Fire," NewsOn6, Dee Duren, Emory Bryan, Nov 19, 2013.

41 "Tulsa woman charged with death of nieces back in custody," Fox23, Angela Hong, Aug 13, 2014.

42 "South Tulsa's London Square Apartments catches fire, 2 children dead, 3 adults injured," Tulsa NBC Channel 2, Nov 18, 2013.

43 Children's aunt arrested after Tulsa fatal apartment fire," *Tulsa World*, Jarrel Wade, Nov 19, 2013.

44 "Police Arrest Aunt of Children Killed in Apartment Fire," CBS Tulsa, NewsOn6, Tulsa, Nov 19, 2013.

45 "Aunt Charged with Murder in Death of Two Children in Tulsa Apartment Fire," NewsOn6, CBS, Tulsa, Nov 26, 2013.

46 "Family of Girls Killed in Tulsa Apartment Fire Socked by Aunt's Murder Charged," CBS, NewsOn6, Tulsa, Nov 26, 2013.

47 ibid.

48 "2015 Oklahoma Police Shootings Total Surpasses Number of Shootings in All of 2014," *Tulsa World*, Sept 24, 2015.

49 Tina Long, London Square tenant interview with author, June 25, 2016.

50 Allen Gorenflo, London Square tenant and electrician interview with author, Sept 7, 2014.

51 "Why Oklahoma has the highest incarceration rate in the country," *Reveal*, Allison Herrera, Feb 13, 2019.

52 "Business community should help women recover," *Tulsa World*, Ed Martinez Jr., Tulsa World Community Advisory Board, Aug 16, 2015."

53 Affidavits signed by Tyrone Coleman, Timothy Jones, Dyanne Coleman, and Chrisandria Moses re: Torrance Williams statements of DA promised leniency.

54 Miashah Moses Preliminary Hearing CF-13-5834, Mar 13, 2014.

55 Tulsa District Court Case #CM-2012-4082, Aug 16, 2012, State of Oklahoma v. Torrance Lamont Williams, bench warrant issued for arrest Apr 24, 2014.

56 "Oklahoma Gets F Grade in 2015 State Integrity Investigation: Special treatment for some shows transparency is skin deep," State Integrity Investigation/Global Integrity, Cary Aspinwall.

57 "Equal access to justice more than just words," *Tulsa World*, David Riggs, Oklahoma Access to Justice Commission, Mar 25, 2019.

58 Tulsa District Court Case #CF-2013-3217, Jul 10, 2013, State of Oklahoma v. Makayla Rhotenberry.

59 "Tulsa Mother Bound Over for Trial in Daughter's Drowning," CBS, NewsOn6, Tulsa, Oct 14, 2013.

60 "Woman gets probation in bathtub drowning of child," *Tulsa World*, Bill Braun, Apr 4, 2014.

61 Sand Springs Police Tracis #14-011008 drowning of child in pool, July 1, 2014.

62 "Police: Toddler Drowns in Pool, "CBS, NewsOn6, Tulsa, Jul 1, 2014.

63 "Tulsa police say 8-mos-old boy survives near drowning incident," ABC, Channel 2, Tulsa, Aug 27, 2014.

64 Tulsa Police TRACIS #2014050596, Aug 27, 2014 report of juvenile near drowning.

65 Interviews with Chrisandria Moses and Keahmiee Moses by author, Apr 28, 2016.

66 Wikipedia, 2015 Shooting of Eric Harris," https://en.wikipedia.org/wiki/2015_shooting_of_Eric_Harris

[67] "Federal inmate charged in Glenpool child-rape case bound over for trial," *Tulsa World*, Amanda Bland, Feb 20, 2015.

[68] "Kevin Smith faces a judge Monday for child porn charges," Fox, Fox23, Tulsa, Sept 15, 2104.

[69] Rape victim statement, Tulsa District Court Case #CG-2014-5435 transcript, Apr 27, 2016.

[70] "Man Sentenced to 120 Years in Rape of Glenpool Girl," CBS Tulsa, NewsOn6, Tulsa, Erin Conrad, Apr 27, 2016.

[71] Email from Cindy Struder, June 2, 2016, former manager London Square, re: problems have turned deadly.

[72] "Chouteau woman gets suspended sentence in DUI-related crash that killed 2-year-old daughter," *Tulsa World*, Paighten Harkins, May 4, 2016.

[73] 21 OK Stat § 21-843.5(B) Child Neglect: Failure to Supervise.

[74] S-2017-580, Oklahoma Supreme Court, Judge Caputo re Steven Wade Jameson, July 2018.

[75] Sharp, Susan F., "Mean Lives, Mean Laws: Oklahoma's Women Prisoners," (Rutgers University Press, New Brunswick, NJ, 2014).

[76] OCSN CF-2013-673 Lachelle v. Oklahoma Bar Journal, Jul 14, 2018.

[77] "Judith Nix sentenced to life for murder of husband," *Tulsa World*, Samantha Vincent, Apr 6, 2017.

[78] "Oklahoma mother gets 10 years for $31 marijuana sale," CBS, Ed Martinez, Feb 23, 2011.

[79] Sharp, Susan F., "Mean Lives, Mean Laws: Oklahoma Women's Prisoners," (Indiana Book Company, Marion, IN, 2014).

80 "Tulsa Equality Indicators Report 2018," Indicator 30: Gender & Arrests re: Oklahoma traditionally leads the nation in arrest rates.

81 "Amber Hilberling case: From her husband's killing at a Tulsa high-rise to her death in a prison cell," *Tulsa World*, June 20, 2017.

82 Elias, J.R., "PUSHED: State of Oklahoma vs. Amber Hilberling," Arabelle Publishing, Santa Rosa Beach, FL (2016).

83 Ibid.

84 "Amber Hilberling discusses her husband's fatal fall on 'Dateline NBC'," *Tulsa World*, May 18, 2013.

85 Jessica Parr interview with auithor, Oklahoma City Correctional Center, May 12, 2019.

86 Elias, J.R., "PUSHED: State of Oklahoma vs. Amber Hilberling," (Arabelle Publishing, Santa Rosa Beach, FL, 2016).

87 "Amber Hilberling's parents tell Dr. Phil their daughter might have been murdered," *Tulsa World*, Corey Jones, Nov 15, 2016.

88 "Oklahoma Corrections Department sued over inmate's suicide," *The Associated Press*, Sept 22, 2018.

89 Elias, J.R. "PUSHED: State of Oklahoma vs. Amber Hilberling," Arabelle Publishing, Santa Rosa Beach, FL (2016).

90 Angela Hong, Fox, Fox23, Tulsa, OK, Chrisandria Moses interview, March 2014.

91 "3 Murders in 10 Months at Oklahoma Prison Run by CCA," *Prison Legal News*, Joe Watson, Jan 3, 2018.

92 "Robert Bates, Oklahoma volunteer cop, found guilty of manslaughter; jury recommends harshest punishment," *New York Daily News*, Alfred Ng, Apr 28, 2016.

93 "Robert Bates, Oklahoma volunteer cop, found guilty of manslaughter; jury recommends harshest punishment," *New York Daily News*, Alfred Ng, Apr 28, 2016.

94 "Tulsa County Settles Eric Harris Lawsuit for $6 Million Days after Robert Bates Renews Appeal," *Tulsa World*, Corey Jones, Mar 10, 2018.

95 "Oklahoma agency investigates apparent Bates parole violation," *Associated Press*, Justin Juazapivicius, May 10, 2018.

96 2018 Tulsa Equality Indicators Report, Indicator 28, 29, & 33 Ratio of Black and White Arrests/Police Use of Force.

97 "Oklahoma agency investigates apparent Bates parole violation," *Associated Press*, Justin Juozapavicius, May 10, 2018.

98 "Manslaughter Charges for Tulsa's Killer Cop," *The Daily Beast*, Kate Briquelet, Feb. 11, 2016.

99 "Tulsa County settles Eric Harris excessive force lawsuit for $6 million days after Robert Bates renews appeal," *Tulsa World*, Corey Jones, Mar 10, 2018.

100 "Oklahoma Gets F Grade in 2015 State Integrity Investigation: Special treatment for some shows transparency is skin deep," State Integrity Investigation/Global Integrity, Cary Aspinwall.

101 "Judge who moonlights as pro wrestler allegedly likes massage parlors," The Lost Ogle, October 18, 2018.

102 "Two felony 'John doe' indictments filed in Tulsa County District Court," *Tulsa World*, Samantha Vincent, Nov 16, 2018.

103 "District Judge James Caputo says he was 'set up,' had never paid a prostitute", *Tulsa World*, Oct 19, 2018, Samantha Vincent.

104 "Tulsa teen says her cop parents should 'rot' after their arrest for boyfriend's murder," *New York Daily News*, Deborah Hastings, Aug 6, 2014.

105 "Shannon Kepler's attorneys still pushing to have new judge…" *Tulsa World*, June 20, 2017, Samantha Vincent.

106 Ibid.

107 "Former Tulsa officer Shannon Kepler to keep pension," *Tulsa World*, Corey Jones, May 25, 2018.

108 "Two Tulsa Men declared innocent in 1994 fatal shooting," *Tulsa World*, Arianna Pickard, May 10, 2016.

109 "Wrongfully convicted Oklahomans among stars of Innocence Project event," *Tulsa World*, Ziva Brandstetter, Sep 27, 2014.

110 "I can't hold no grudge. Life's too short," *Tulsa World*, Samantha Vincent, Jul 17, 2019.

111 Ibid.

112 "Lawsuit: Police Used Coercion and Hid Evidence to Wrongfully Convict Seven People," *Daily Beast*, July 14, 2017, Kate Briquelet.

113 "Former Tulsa homicide sergeant Mike Huff among Law Enforcement Hall of Fame inductees," *Tulsa World*, Stephen Pingry, Jan 2, 2019.

114 Ibid.

115 U.S. District Court for the Northern District of Oklahoma, Case No. 12-CV-282-JED-JFJ, Larita Barnes v. United States of America.

116 "Woman freed in TPD corruption probe wins $5 million judgment," *Tulsa World*, Curtis Killman Feb 18, 2020.

117 "Will government be forced to pay Tula woman who was framed by law enforcement?" *Tulsa World*, Nov 10, 2018, Curtis Killman.

118 U.S. District Court for the Northern District of Oklahoma, Case No. 12-CV-282-JED-JFJ, Larita Barnes v. United States of America.

119 2018 Tulsa Equality Indicators Report, Indicator 28, 29, & 33 Ratio of Black and White Arrests/Police Use of Force.

120 "TPD sergeant testifies DA 'disrespectful' when he brought charges against Shelby," *The Frontier*, Kassie McClung, May 12, 2017.

121 Ibid.

122 "That 'Bad Dude' Tulsa Police Gunned Down 'Was a Father,' a 'Son' and a Student," *Mother Jones*, Sept 21, 2016, Brandon E. Patterson.

123 Ibid.

124 "Terence Crutcher's sister defends him from police officer's claim that he was a "bad dude," *VOX*, German Lopez, Jan 20, 2016.

125 "Increasingly emotional Betty Shelby shown in dramatic video interview with investigators," *The Frontier*, May 11 2017, Dylan Goforth.

126 "Fired Tulsa police officer hired as detention officer in Rogers County," *Tulsa World*, Stetson Payne, Oct 2, 2019

127 "2018 Tulsa Equality Indicators Report." https://www.tulsaei.org/webdocs/Tulsa_Equality_Indicators_Annual_Report_2018_Web.pdf

128 "First Equality Indicators meeting on racial and gender disparities set for June 26," *Tulsa World*, Apr 25, 2019, Kevin Canfield.

129 "City Leaders Dispute Motive of TPD Internal Investigation," CBS Tulsa, NewsOn6, March 11, 219, Lori Fulbright.

130 "Police video show confusion in wake of alleged stabbing of Tulsa district court judge," *Enid News Eagle* reprint from *The Frontier*, Dylan Goforth, Mar 221, 2019.

131 "Ice Hides Body in condominium's Pond," *Oklahoman*, Feb. 1, 1987, Archive ID; 295891.

132 Robin Simmons interview with author, Feb 29, 2020.

133 Earleen Simmons interview, May 11, 2019.

134 "City's search for unmarked graves from the 1921 race massacre should go on," *Tulsa World*, Editorial Writers, Dec 15, 2019.

135 "Tulsa Race Massacre burial committee to get report on mass grave search," *Tulsa World,* Randy Krehbiel, Dec 16, 2019.

136 "1921 Race Riot: Tribute mystery unsolved," *Tulsa World*, Randy Krehbiel, May 31, 2002 Updated May 21, 2020.

137 Ibid.

138 "They was killing black people," *The Wall Street Journal*, DeNeen L. Brown, Sept 28, 2018.

139 Ibid.

140 "Longstanding distrust, anger revealed in hunt for Tulsa Race Massacre graves," *Tulsa World*, Randy Krehbiel, Mar 3, 2020.

141 "Come home 'A.L.I.V.E." *Tulsa Voice*, Jezy J. Gray, Mar 6, 2019, based on book "Daddy, Did You Hear the News?" by Sonya Whittaker Gragg, MSW (2018).

142 "America's Other Family-Separation Crisis," *New York Magazine*, Sarah Stillman, Nov 5, 2018.

CPSIA information can be obtained
at www.ICGtesting.com
Printed in the USA
JSHW041157071220
10044JS00002B/69